JESUS AND THE
GOSPEL WOMEN

Joanna Collicutt McGrath

First published in Great Britain in 2009

Society for Promoting Christian Knowledge
36 Causton Street
London SW1P 4ST

British Library Cataloguing-in-Publication Data
A catalogue record for this book is available from the British Library

ISBN 978–0–281–06022–1

1 3 5 7 9 10 8 6 4 2

Typeset by Graphicraft Ltd, Hong Kong
Printed in Great Britain by Ashford Colour Press

Produced on paper from sustainable forests

In loving memory of my grandmother,
Agnes Shannon Collicutt, who was the
first to tell me that Joanna was a disciple of Jesus

Contents

———•◆•———

Contents

Acknowledgements

The idea for this book emerged from a weekend retreat that I conducted for the women of the Church of St John and St Philip, The Hague, in the spring of 2005. I owe an enormous debt of gratitude for their hospitality and responsiveness, and especially to Rosie Dymond, who first encouraged me to write it. I would also like to thank Felix and Charles Prescott for their unflagging enthusiastic support.

I have gained helpful insights from conversations with Brendan Callaghan, Annie Cooper, Nicholas Coulton, Jill and Jeremy Duff, Julie Elsworth, Miri Keen, Alister McGrath, Paul McGrath, Martin Poulsom, Georgie Simpson, Henry Wansbrough and Fraser Watts.

My students at Heythrop College teach me at least as much as I teach them. I would like to express especial thanks to Alice Herron, Catherine Inglesby and Sahaya G. Selvam.

Alison Barr at SPCK has been a model of patience and wise advice as the project lengthened beyond what either of us had initially envisaged.

Finally, the long-suffering people of the Parish of Witney have allowed me to explore many of the ideas in this book with them Sunday by Sunday in my sermons, with good humour, patience and grace. I trust we have grown together in the process.

Introduction

<hr/>

Jesus and his women

'Then he went up on to the mountain side, and called to him those whom it pleased him to call; so they came to him.' There it all was, the history of my life, of my whole vocation; above all, of the special claims that Jesus makes on my soul.[1]

This book is about Jesus and his women – his encounters with women, his discourses on women as recorded in the four Gospels, and his relationship with women today. But though it is written primarily with women in mind, and will engage with the stories[2] of gospel women, aiming to make connections with the lives of today's women, its primary focus is the divine man *Jesus*.

It is a book that is intended to feed the spiritual life of women, but I hope that male readers will also find it helpful. After all, over the centuries women have appropriated, learned from and grown through stories about Jesus and his men. The quotation that opens this book is a good example. It refers to a biblical account of the call of the twelve male disciples,[3] but it is written by a woman, St Thérèse of the Child Jesus (1873–97). It came quite naturally to Thérèse, in the light of her own experience, to assume that it pleased Jesus to call people like her – *women* – to him, and she appropriated the story from Mark's Gospel accordingly. In this she is surely correct. For biblical accounts of the way Jesus met with men are not *ipso facto* accounts of the way he didn't meet with women.

In the same way, the relationship between Jesus and his women is a special case of the relationship between Jesus and his people. And this special case, while in some respects distinctive, is not 'other' or inferior. It stands alongside the relationship between Jesus and his men as an equally valid model or prototype for Christian discipleship and ministry. For biblical accounts of the way Jesus met with women are not *ipso facto* accounts of the way he didn't meet with men.

Despite the emphasis on women, this book is not driven by a feminist agenda, though it does draw on insights from feminist scholars at several points. Feminism refers to a collection of movements that criticize patriarchal structures, attitudes and practices from within. My cultural background is located somewhere a little different, and is perhaps best described as matrifocal.[4] On my mother's side I come from one of the very few societies in the world that has a claim to being a matriarchy, the Khasi people of the Indian state of Meghalaya.[5] So my perspective on patriarchy, including Western and Near Eastern Judaeo-Christian patriarchy, has always been more that of the perplexed outsider than the oppressed insider. For good or ill, patriarchy is not in my blood, and this is bound to affect the way that I receive and communicate the gospel texts.

Little girl, get up!

The phrase 'gospel women' refers to the women whose stories are recorded in the four biblical documents we know as the Gospels. But it can also be understood as referring to all women who have received the gospel (good news) of Jesus Christ. This naturally invites the question of what this gospel is, especially in relation to women. What is it that makes it such good news?

I have spent several years reflecting on what the take-home message of the gospel is for people of our generation, and indeed for all generations and cultures. Because I am a psychologist it comes naturally to me to think in terms of the psychological needs (literally 'soul-needs') of human beings.

Introduction

I have come to the conclusion that the message that touches the heart (rather than the head) of those who respond to the gospel falls into three parts:

- 'You are not on your own.' (Immanuel)
- 'Things don't have to be this way.' (The offer of salvation)
- 'Get up and grow up!' (Being raised with Christ)

The first provides assurance of security; the second offers realistic options for change, and thus hope; the third makes demands, but also gives affirmation. I will come back to these three themes from time to time through the book. For now, I want to concentrate on the idea of 'getting up'.

The Greek verbs used in the New Testament for 'get up' are *egeirō* (e.g. Matthew 17.7) and *anistēmi* (e.g. Luke 15.18). Both verbs are ambiguous, and their dual meaning is well captured in the older English Bible translations that use the word 'arise'. They can either mean a simple move from lying or sitting to standing, or they can mean rising from death to life. These two meanings come together in the Christian understanding of being raised with Christ. Getting up – arising – involves a move from passive to active, from relaxed to alert, from weak to strong, from sick to well, from dead to alive, from 'the world below' to 'the world above' (John 8.23), and – perhaps most of all – from lowly to exalted status.

Being raised with Christ is about becoming fully human, reaching our God-given potential, and therefore becoming truly adult. It involves a direction of movement from a simple child–parent relationship with God to a child–parent *and* adult–adult relationship with God. Christ's work of creation has endowed us with the status of children made in the image of God (even if we do not understand or claim this status). His work of redemption has offered us the possibility of an adult–adult relationship with God.

So, the call of Jesus to an adolescent girl, preserved by Christian tradition as his spoken Aramaic words '*Talitha cum*'

(Mark 5.41), is a prototype for the call of the Christian disciple: 'Get up! And have a chance to grow up!' I will explore this idea in more depth in Chapter 6. I introduce this nameless young woman now because her story (Mark 5.23, 35–43 and parallels) is foundational and inspirational for all gospel women, and thus for this book.

As we have seen, getting up – arising – entails a change of status. In their relationship with Jesus Christ the status of individual women is raised, not abased. The little girl indeed gets up (Mark 5.42 and parallels); the widow at the Temple (Mark 12.41–44; Luke 21.1–4) and the woman who washes Jesus' feet (Mark 14.3–9 and parallels) are held up as examples of piety; the woman with chronic bleeding moves from the sick role that excludes her from public life to a central role among 'the people' (Luke 8.47); the woman with curvature of the spine literally stands tall for the first time in 18 years (Luke 13.11–13); the Samaritan woman at the well becomes known not for her chaotic lifestyle but for her evangelism (John 4.39); the Syro-Phoenician woman wins the argument with Jesus (Mark 7.29); a group of women led by Mary Magdalene are commissioned as primary witnesses of the resurrection (Matthew 28.7 and parallels); and above all there is Mary of Nazareth, an obscure young girl who becomes the Lord's servant (Luke 1.38), a representative of his people Israel.

What does Mary do after she has styled herself 'the Lord's servant'? She immediately gets up (*anastasa*) (Luke 1.39), and shortly after this she sings a triumphant song about her experience of being raised up. The song treats the raising of Mary as a prototype for and sign of God's raising of all his people:[6]

> My soul praises the Lord, and my spirit rejoices in God my
> Saviour, for he has looked respectfully on the humiliation
> of his servant.
> Look! From now on everyone will consider me fortunate;
> for the Mighty One has accomplished great things for me, and
> his name is holy.

And his mercy is for those who revere him from generation to
generation.

He has done a mighty deed with his arm; he has scattered the
arrogant in the purposes of their hearts.

He has taken down the rulers from their thrones, and raised
up those of low status; he has filled those who are hungry
with good things, and those who are rich he has sent away
empty handed.

He has taken his child Israel in hand, remembering mercy,
according to his promise to our fathers, to Abraham and to
his descendants forever.

(Luke 1.46–55)

As we shall see, this raising of women doesn't always come
about through their sitting and waiting, like Walt Disney's
Snow White, for their prince to come. It can sometimes come
through their assertive request for, or even seizure of, what
they understand as their due. If this last point seems strange or
even troubling it may be because our models of Christian faith
are skewed and less than biblical. Our assumptions about the
nature of faith may be too cognitive and insufficiently enactive,
too rational and insufficiently emotional.

The Gospels do not tell us stories of people who sit at home
and, having thought long and hard about Jesus, come to the
disinterested conclusion that he is God incarnate. They tell
us of people who go out to find Jesus, who break into houses
where Jesus is a guest, or who call to Jesus from the wayside.
Jesus describes many of these people as showing great faith.
They are to a man and woman desperate people, people who
may perhaps have had an intellectual curiosity about Jesus, but
whose main thoughts are that Jesus might be able to do something for them. The strength of their belief, the energy that
impels them to seek him, is fuelled in part by wishful thinking.
For if Jesus cannot help them, they know there is no help for
them. Some are more dignified than others in their approach;
the centurion from Capernaum (Matthew 8.5–10) is perhaps

the most dignified, and blind Bartimaeus (Mark 10.46–52) the least. But all are desperate, and all take some sort of direct action.

When Jesus tells such people that their faith has healed them or those they love, it is their desperate action, their assertive request, their bringing of themselves to him that he is commending. This is in part what he is referring to when he talks of people forcing their way into the kingdom (Matthew 11.12; Luke 16.16),[7] and it is what he is commending when he instructs his disciples to approach God in trust with open hands (Matthew 7.7–11; Luke 11.9–13).

On the whole, gospel women are like this. They are highly assertive creatures, who simply bring who they are to their encounters with Jesus. The gospel writers tell us that other people sometimes had an issue with this (Matthew 15.23; Luke 7.39; John 4.27), but that it was generally not a problem for Jesus.

As we begin to engage with some of the biblical texts about Jesus and women we will find that we too have our issues, and these may make some of the texts seem jarring and problematic. If they do strike us as uncomfortable, this is a healthy sign. Part of the job of the biblical texts is to get under our skin and make us think and rethink what we know about Jesus and about ourselves. Sometimes the texts will seem inconsistent or even frankly contradictory. Again, if this troubles us and encourages us repeatedly to come back to them, it is no bad thing. It is only if these texts about Jesus and women strike us as bland, overfamiliar and irrelevant that we should be worried. In that case perhaps our own issues are so significant that we may be shutting our ears to what they have to say to us.

This is one of the reasons why most of the New Testament texts quoted in this book are my own translations. I have chosen to present as near to a literal translation as possible. My aim has been to allow the texts to speak in a fresh and indeed strange[8] way to us – to help them dislodge our assumptions or touch our hidden issues. The disadvantage of this approach is that the translations lack elegance, and at times may read as clumsy, in which case the reader is encouraged to reread the relevant passage in the New Revised Standard Version. All Old Testament texts are from the NRSV.

But this book does not begin with the strange text of the Bible. Chapter 1 is concerned with the more familiar, comfortable and delicious territory of *Pride and Prejudice* and its hero, Mr Darcy.

1

Beyond Mr Darcy

———◆———

I need a hero

I'm really in love with Jesus. I think deep down I've always wanted a hero to come into my life and save me and take me on a mad crazy adventure. Now I've got one and I love it.[1]

There is no doubt that for many women Jesus can be a potent hero figure. This may feed their faith in a healthy and life-giving way. But it may also mean that they get stuck in certain patterns of relating to Jesus that can make it difficult to get up and move on. It is therefore worth exploring what it is that makes 'Jesus the hero' so compelling.

A good place to begin is with the work of the analytic psychologist Carl Jung (1875–1961). Jung was interested in features of human psychology that hold true across all cultures and ages. On the basis of his observations of a wide range of human cultures he developed the notion of the 'collective unconscious'. Like Freud before him, Jung thought that there are powerful unconscious processes at work in the psychology of each individual. Like Freud, he thought that these processes are influenced by the individual's experience, particularly during childhood. But Jung's new development was the idea that these unconscious processes have a strong tendency to operate around certain themes. These themes are shaped by the individual's genetic endowment as a member of the human race. That is, there is a part of the unconscious that is essentially the same for all human beings, no matter what their culture or life experience. This is the collective unconscious.[2]

The way that a person's collective unconscious is expressed will, of course, be determined by her particular culture and situation. But, according to Jung, it is possible to dig under this particular surface expression in any individual to reveal a deeper layer that is common to all human beings.[3] This layer is evident in the images and themes found in the myths of all human cultures. (I use the term 'myth' here in its technical sense of a sacred story or grand narrative, which may or may not be based on real events.[4]) Jung argues that the predisposition to form universal mythic images and themes, and to use them as a perspective on the world, is a core characteristic of human psychology. The deep psychic structures underlying them he refers to as 'archetypes'. One broad class of archetype is 'the hero'.

Now it seems that all cultures tell stories of heroes and adventure. Many sacred stories involve heroes who set out on quests marked by an initial call, a struggle and a final victory.[5] The Christian story is no exception. It is arguably the greatest of all hero myths. The Christian Church, psychologically constrained by its collective unconscious, has received Jesus as a hero. That is certainly how I received Jesus as a young woman, and in some ways how I continue to receive him. My worship of the Christian God has been, to a large extent, hero worship of Jesus.

Indeed, Jesus seems to make a very good hero. In her 1986 book *The Hero Within*[6] the literary scholar Carol Pearson delineates six archetypes within the hero umbrella:

- the orphan
- the wanderer
- the warrior
- the altruist
- the innocent
- the magician.

It is clear that such categories influenced the first Christians as they tried to make sense of Jesus and then transmitted his story to future generations. One way in which they did this was to make connections between Jesus and 'types' in the Hebrew Scriptures: people such as David (the warrior), Moses (the wanderer) and Elijah (the magician). These 'types' already conform to the general hero archetype, and so as Jesus is connected with them his hero status is massively reinforced.

Furthermore, as the writer to the Hebrews intimates, Jesus is a far better hero than those who have gone before. He is a superhero.

Unlike David, Moses and Elijah, his story expresses all the hero archetypes on Pearson's list. There are some illustrative examples in Table 1 on page 4.

We all seem to need heroes. They do psychological work on our behalf.[7] Their stories offer us hope of transcending our limitations, especially if the heroes have human weaknesses with which we can identify. They also provide models to show us the way. If we can appropriate their stories we can gain a sense of liberation or protection from dark forces of chaos and malevolence that sometimes threaten to overwhelm us.[8] Last year I was helped through what seemed a very long post-operative recovery period, troubled by fragmented memories of the procedure, and depressed by the effects of the anaesthetic, by reading J. R. R. Tolkien's *The Lord of the Rings*.[9] My barely conscious mantra became, 'If they could get through this, so can I.'

But Selena Gray, the young woman quoted at the beginning of this chapter, doesn't seem to be comparing Jesus so much with a hobbit as with Indiana Jones. Her statement is clearly erotic in content and tone. She is talking about a *romantic* hero. She wants to follow Jesus; she knows he can help her, but she also desires him and presumably hopes or feels that he reciprocates that desire at some level.

A relational erotic approach to Jesus is by no means exclusive to twenty-first-century women. It is, for instance, a dominant

Table 1 The heroic archetype and Jesus

The orphan	'Jesus was about thirty years old when he began his work. He was the son (as was thought) of Joseph' (Luke 3.23, NRSV).
The wanderer	'Foxes have holes, and birds of the air have nests; but the Son of Man has nowhere to lay his head' (Matthew 8.20; Luke 9.58, NRSV).
The warrior	'Jesus said to him, "Away with you, Satan! for it is written, 'Worship the Lord your God, and serve only him.'" Then the devil left him, and suddenly angels came and waited on him' (Matthew 4.10, NRSV).
The altruist	'. . . the Son of Man came not to be served but to serve, and to give his life a ransom for many' (Matthew 20.28; Mark 10.45, NRSV).
The innocent	'When the centurion saw what had taken place, he praised God and said, "Certainly this man was innocent"' (Luke 23.47, NRSV).
The magician	'So the chief priests and the Pharisees called a meeting of the council, and said, "What are we to do? This man is performing many signs. If we let him go on like this, everyone will believe in him . . ."' (John 11.47–48a, NRSV).

theme in the fourth Gospel and in the writings of Paul. But the *romancing* of Jesus the hero is not characteristic of the Bible. The romantic hero has more recent origins in twelfth-century Europe. It was in the literature of the medieval period that romantic love and heroism became intricately linked. The heroes of medieval epics were often on a noble quest for true love that continued to elude them, and on the way they acquired moral virtues and prowess as warriors. In these tales, frequently set to music and performed by troubadours, the hero is the agent and the lady he desires is the object of his affections.

In the nineteenth century the romantic hero begins to be presented from a different perspective. Female writers weave tales whose intended audience is primarily female. The tale is told from the point of view of a female protagonist and the hero is presented as the object (or quasi object) of her affections. The definitive example of this sort of hero is Mr Rochester of Charlotte Brontë's *Jane Eyre*. But there is another hero, similar in many key respects to Mr Rochester, but who has weathered the passage of time rather better. He is Jane Austen's Mr Darcy, the hero of *Pride and Prejudice*, and it is to Mr Darcy we now turn.

The perfect man?

In 2003 Mr Darcy came top in a poll conducted by the Orange Prize for Fiction in which 1,900 women, of all ages, were asked the question, 'Which character from literature would you most like to take you out on a date?' This poll came a full eight years after the phenomenally popular BBC television adaptation of *Pride and Prejudice*, starring Colin Firth, and its results indicate that the Mr Darcy effect is strangely enduring. It cannot simply be attributed to the infamous, inauthentic and yet iconic 'wet shirt scene' of that particular BBC dramatization. Perhaps there are archetypal factors at work here.

Austen was clearly writing about a society in which the options for women without personal fortune (that is, the vast majority) were highly restricted. It was a society within which women were almost exclusively dependent for their physical survival on the protection of a male relative or guardian. Their main aim in life was to secure this protection. The situation depicted at the start of *Pride and Prejudice* is desperate. We are presented with a family of five respectable young women with no fortune and little in the way of male protection. Their mother, Mrs Bennet, is quite rightly obsessed with remedying the situation. Her role in the story is crucial because she repeatedly brings to our attention the fact that her daughters are a short step from destitution. She is a figure of ridicule because of the vulgar and public way in which she expresses her hopes and fears. But these fears are valid, and her attempts to secure wealthy husbands for her daughters are, if clumsily executed, perfectly reasonable.

The story is all about power and its reversal. It is about the powerless second daughter Elizabeth, not blessed with the pre-eminent position and dazzling beauty of her older sister, who nevertheless manages to bring the immensely powerful Mr Darcy under her power by stint of her wits. Of course, Elizabeth Bennet is not vulgar like her mother, but she is more ambitious. Though not fully conscious of what she is doing, she is out to get a man who can secure her a place in the world that will allow her to be herself, not merely guarantee her physical survival. She doesn't just want someone who will offer her salvation (a Mr Collins), she wants someone who will offer her liberation. So, she is extremely choosy about suitors. She is also highly skilled, and the process of claiming Mr Darcy's attention is carried out so fluently and unconsciously that when he finally expresses interest in her she is genuinely surprised.

Austen's novels usually include an anti-heroine. In *Pride and Prejudice* this role is taken by the unpleasant Miss Bingley. The anti-heroine is also in pursuit of the hero, but lacks subtlety, and is usually humiliated for her pains. She is basically a loser. Austen is not deriding such women for pursuing men (especially if they are poor), but for their lack of skill at playing the game. Women in this society do what they have to do in order to survive (this is made clear through the sympathetic portrayal of Charlotte Lucas who enters into a loveless marriage with Mr Collins), and they may often be acting in the interests of dependent relatives.

Elizabeth is in a sense bearing the burden of her whole family, her younger sisters and ageing parents. By securing Darcy she is securing their future as well as her own. Because she is not a conventional beauty she does not at first attract the positive attention of Darcy, but through her pert intelligent observations and assertively demure behaviour she finally manages it. She does what she has to do for her own sake and the sake of her family. In this she bears more than a passing resemblance to the Syro-Phoenician woman of Mark's Gospel, to whom we shall return in Chapter 2.

But what of Mr Darcy? What makes him so special? Towards the end of the book, in a playful conversation with her sister, Elizabeth speaks of the growth of her love for Darcy: 'It has been coming on so gradually, that I hardly know when it began. But I believe I must date it from my first seeing his beautiful grounds at Pemberley.'

Darcy has inherited from his father, in addition to a substantial income of 'ten thousand a year', a vast mansion with many rooms. Here we see something interesting. For while what is happening with Darcy is fictional and its scale parochial, this is the first of several striking parallels with the real and cosmic story of Jesus. Both Jesus and Darcy have potent, loving and essentially absent fathers whose deeds are recalled with awe and affection, and into whose house they can welcome those whom they love:

> How lovely is your dwelling-place,
>   O LORD of hosts!
> My soul longs, indeed it faints
>   for the courts of the LORD;
> my heart and my flesh sing for joy
>   to the living God.
>
> Even the sparrow finds a home,
>   and the swallow a nest for herself,
>   where she may lay her young,
> at your altars, O LORD of hosts,
>   my King and my God.
>   (Psalm 84.1–3, NRSV)

In my father's house there are many rooms. If it were not, would I have said to you that I go to prepare a place for you?
                    (John 14.2a)

The second parallel is that of innocence and silence. Darcy is disliked and shunned by many, subjected to false and unsubstantiated accusations at the hands of Mr Wickham (the villain) and for much of the plot says nothing to justify himself:

> He was oppressed, and he was afflicted,
>> yet he did not open his mouth;
> like a lamb that is led to the slaughter,
>> and like a sheep that before its shearers is silent,
>> so he did not open his mouth.
>
> (Isaiah 53.7, NRSV)

Part of what fuels Elizabeth's love for Darcy is her late realization that she has, through her naivety, been a party to his persecution. Yet he was all the time innocent, and indeed all the time acted out of love for her: 'She grew absolutely ashamed of herself . . . "How despicably have I acted!" she cried, "I, who have prided myself on my discernment! . . . How humiliating is this discovery! Yet, how just a humiliation! . . . Till this moment I never knew myself." '

> Who was the guilty? Who brought this upon Thee?
> Alas, my treason, Jesus hath undone Thee!
> 'Twas I, Lord Jesus, I it was denied Thee:
> I crucified Thee.[10]

Elizabeth seems to go through something akin to a 'conviction of sin'.[11] She is brought low in her own eyes, but strangely life seems to offer more hope because the nobility of conduct that she has witnessed in Darcy elevates the whole enterprise. She is both ashamed and inspired.

The third parallel is perhaps the most significant. Darcy, acting out of love for Elizabeth, secretly pays his enemy, Wickham, a very costly ransom to save her and her undeserving family from utter degradation and destitution. The ransom, or more correctly financial inducement for marriage, is beyond anything the Bennets could ever have afforded. It restores their status as respectable folk through a covering of the shame of their wayward daughter Lydia, and moreover guarantees her future security. The family is raised up at Darcy's expense.

Elizabeth's love is thus further fuelled by gratitude, and the following speech signals her final acceptance of Darcy's suit:

> 'Mr Darcy, I am a very selfish creature; and for the sake of giving relief to my own feelings, care not how much I may be wounding yours. I can no longer help thanking you for your unexampled kindness to my poor sister. Ever since I have known it, I have been most anxious to acknowledge to you how gratefully I feel it.'

> 'A certain moneylender had two debtors, one owing five hundred denarii, the other fifty. As they were not in a position to pay, he cancelled both their debts. So which of them will love him more?' In answer Simon said, 'I suppose the one for whom he cancelled more.' And he said to him, 'You have judged rightly.' And having turned towards the woman, he said to Simon, 'Do you see this woman? . . . her cancelled sins were many since she loves so much.'   (Luke 7.41–44a, 47a)

> > Therefore, kind Jesus, since I cannot pay thee,
> > I do adore thee, and will ever pray thee,
> > think on thy pity and thy love unswerving,
> > not my deserving.[12]

The combination of the innocence of the suffering hero with his costly and unmerited love gift is a heady cocktail, almost guaranteed to call up intense devotion on the part of she who receives his love. And this devotion has in its turn the effect of securing an attachment to the powerful hero, a receipt of all his benefits by association, and a dramatic raising of status. At the end of *Pride and Prejudice* Elizabeth becomes Mrs Darcy, mistress of Pemberley, and a member of a family whose social status far outranks her own. The Christian parallel can be seen in she who responds to the grace of God in Christ with intense devotion and discovers what it means to be in Christ, to participate with Christ in both his sufferings and his exaltation.

When contemporary women describe Jesus as their hero they are perhaps tuning in to those features of the Jesus story that make Mr Darcy so compelling and desirable. There is something about a potent, wealthy, noble, misunderstood, suffering and altruistic man that makes him devastatingly attractive to women. But the clincher in the case of Mr Darcy is something else. It is his *mystery*. Darcy is remote, rarely speaks but seems always to be watching Elizabeth, displays little emotion,[13] broods rather a lot, and for much of the book is absent (though not necessarily inactive). For Elizabeth all this makes him hard to read, and the courtship as difficult as it is delicious. For the twenty-first-century reader, however, it offers the possibility of projection. The spare account of Darcy, the sense that he has hidden depths and smouldering fires beneath the enigmatic surface, allows the reader to project her ideals, her needs and her fantasies on to him. So it is with Jesus.

From hero to idol

We are not told what Darcy says when Elizabeth finally accepts his understated proposal of marriage: 'The happiness which this reply produced, was such as he had probably never felt before; and he expressed himself on the occasion as sensibly and as warmly as a man violently in love can be supposed to do.' In one way this seems like a let-down, but Austen is cleverly inviting the reader to 'suppose' what a wonderful man who is violently in love might say and do. There is thus no room for disappointment; there is little room for reality, but there is room for that inexpressible, even inconceivable something that is 'beyond my wildest dreams'. Control of Darcy is offered to the reader, and he may thus become her mental plaything.

Just like Mr Darcy, Jesus of Nazareth is a mystery who invites projection. The Gospels present Jesus as not just enigmatic but frankly secretive at times. Their accounts of the personality of Jesus are spare and minimal. There is hardly anything to them. They are not even consistent with each other (at least on first reading). Yet we can read the Gospels and feel that we know Jesus well. More than that, we can come to love him deeply. We are psychologically inclined to smooth out the inconsistencies, and to fill in the gaps. We may do this, quite unconsciously, to fit in with our starting assumptions – 'I know that Jesus was a heroic man' – or to meet our emotional desires – 'I need a hero'.

Sometimes the process is completely conscious:

> I find this [a belief in the atoning effect of his own death] not only a strange notion, but an unattractive notion to attribute to Jesus. *I don't want* Jesus to have seen his own death as having . . . [this] significance . . . As a Christian, *I want Jesus to be an attractive figure.*[14]

This human tendency to turn Jesus into the man we want him to be was masterfully documented by Albert Schweitzer (1875–1965) in his book *The Quest of the Historical Jesus*,[15] which gives an account of a series of attempts to construct a definitive personality portrait of Jesus. These found their expression in a number of 'Lives of Jesus'[16] that were published in the nineteenth century, influenced by (among other things) the rise of the novel as a distinctive literary genre. Schweitzer demonstrated that Jesus was idealized in each work in such a way as to fit the ethical assumptions and aspirations of its particular author.

We cannot help but project our core assumptions, pet theories, unresolved hurts and deep yearnings on to the figure of Jesus. Moreover, as we have seen, the gospel texts seem almost to invite this. We do it to an extent in all our human relationships, and this side of the grave we will not be free of the tendency to construct reality according to our own agenda.

11

It is part of what it means to be human. Indeed the incarnation involves Christ's willing subjection to this process by becoming not a divine mind inhabiting a human body, but a fully human mind-body that entered into relationship with other human beings.[17] And, as we have seen, human minds seem to throw up the need for a hero, especially when times are hard or life seems empty:

Where have all the good men gone
And where are all the gods?
Where's the street-wise Hercules
To fight the rising odds?

Isn't there a white knight upon a fiery steed?
Late at night I toss and I turn and I dream of what I need

Somewhere after midnight
In my wildest fantasy
Somewhere just beyond my reach
There's someone reaching back for me

Racing on the thunder and rising with the heat
It's gonna take a superman to sweep me off my feet

Up where the mountains meet the heavens above
Out where the lightning splits the sea
I could swear there is someone somewhere
Watching me

Through the wind and the chill and the rain
And the storm and the flood
I can feel his approach
Like a fire in my blood

I need a hero
I'm holding out for a hero 'til the end of the night
He's gotta be strong
And he's gotta be fast
And he's gotta be fresh from the fight.[18]

This commercially very successful song was made famous in the 1990s by Bonnie Tyler. It may at first seem surprising that a piece of light eroticism should have such an apocalyptic tone. It could almost be a call to the Christ who is 'coming on the clouds' (Revelation 1.7). Yet this is actually rather what we should expect if we accept Jung's notion of the collective unconscious; all our yearnings and experiences are organized around a limited number of recurring themes. Nevertheless, the song differs significantly from the Christian spiritual tradition in one key respect. The last stanza (which is actually a repeated refrain) makes it very clear that the woman who is awaiting or invoking her hero intends to control him. He exists to meet her needs, and must ('gotta') possess certain characteristics – strength, speed and victory. He probably won't say much. His task is to deliver the goods. In this he resembles the version of Mr Darcy constructed by many female consumers of *Pride and Prejudice* – a pseudo-agent who is in fact an object or plaything.

We need to take care that we do not treat Jesus our hero in this way. Acknowledging the reality that human beings naturally approach the enigmatic figure of Jesus with their own agendas does not give us the licence to view him solely as an object to be possessed or used to advance these agendas. If we do this we move from hero worship to idol worship. Fortunately, Jesus himself helps us here. For he has two advantages over Mr Darcy – Jesus is both a real historical figure and a continuing living presence.

The experience of those who engage at all seriously with Jesus is that if they try to treat him as a plaything, he instead responds as a playmate;[19] if they try to objectify him he responds by moving into the driving seat. While Jesus can clearly be considered a hero, and this adds to his allure, he seems to turn the concept inside out and redefine it. As he acquiesces with our categories or archetypes we find that he is

13

subverting them. This is one of the few reliable things that can be said about the 'personality' of Jesus. He seems familiar and comfortable and then he springs a surprise, if not a shock, that moves us on to unexpected places (hence the sense of adventure described by Selena Gray). This process is beautifully described in Revelation 5 by John of Patmos who, like Bonnie Tyler, is holding out for a hero:

> And I saw in the right hand of the one sitting on the throne a scroll that had been written on the inside and on the outside, sealed with seven seals; and I saw a mighty angel proclaiming in a loud voice, 'Who is worthy to open the scroll and to break its seals?' And no one was able in heaven, or on earth or under the earth, to open the scroll, or to look inside it. And I was weeping deeply because no one was found worthy to open the scroll or to look inside it. (Revelation 5.1–4)

Then it looks as if the hero will materialize, and he will be strong, fast and fresh from the fight:

> And one of the elders said to me, 'Don't cry. Look, the conquering Lion of the tribe of Judah, the Root of David, is to open the scroll and its seven seals.' (Revelation 5.5)

Finally, the hero is revealed:

> Then I saw in the middle of the throne and the four living creatures, and among the elders, a Lamb standing as if it had been slaughtered. (Revelation 5.6a)

The hero turns out to be a weak, immobile, loser.

In coming to the Jesus who is presented to us from four quite distinct perspectives in the Gospels, it is important to be aware that we have certain expectations that he will challenge, and certain desires that he may meet in unexpected ways. Women in particular may have a tendency to turn Jesus into the sort of romantic hero who can become an idol.[20] This is for external sociological reasons as much as internal psychological ones. Heroes appeal to disempowered groups, and women have a cultural inheritance, if not also a present reality, of disempowerment.[21]

Heroes tell us that we are not on our own, and that things don't have to stay the way they are. Romantic heroes save us, solve our problems and sweep us off our feet, with little effort required on our part. Idols require even less of us. A relationship with a hero may ease pain and bring comfort or excitement, and it might be quite a good place to start with Jesus, who after all brings us the good news that with God we are indeed not on our own and that things certainly don't have to stay the way they are. But we need also to allow Jesus to help us get beyond this, to hear his call to 'Get up!', to accept that his type of heroics may not easily fit with what we want or expect, and to be prepared to be heroes ourselves.

So, in this book I aim to explore the gospel texts about Jesus and women not so much from the perspective of what women (or men) need or want, not in terms of the personal stories of gospel women, not in terms of received Christological categories, but from the perspective of the divine man Jesus himself. That is, I want as far as it is possible in any human sense, to let the Jesus who reveals himself through the gospel texts set the agenda, and to cultivate an attitude of accurate empathy and real listening to his words and actions as they are set down by each gospel writer.

Of course, despite my best intentions my own wants and needs will inevitably be part of the process. It will probably be obvious to the reader that I am a woman, a psychologist, with some sympathy to feminism, and above all someone who is fascinated by the humanity of Jesus of Nazareth. However, I will try not to foreground only those aspects of the gospel portraits of Jesus that appeal to me, nor to harmonize genuine tensions and contradictions in the texts. After all, real people are full of contradictions and tensions; real people are known in different ways to the different people in their lives; real people behave with apparent inconsistency on different occasions.

The book does not start with Jesus the object of our adoration, but with Jesus the agent who engages with us. Each chapter looks at significant aspects of the psychology of Jesus as it is expressed in his engagement with women. This psychology is not about his personality traits and temperament – questions such as, 'Was Jesus an extravert?' are anachronistic and probably meaningless. Rather it is about the definitive or characteristic ways in which, we are told, Jesus of Nazareth saw, thought about, communicated and acted in relationship with women.

This Jesus-centred approach does not, however, relegate the women of the Gospels to the role of supporting acts or passive spectators. The gospel accounts tell of negotiated two-way transactions between Jesus and women. It soon becomes clear that, alongside a giving of himself, Jesus makes demands and even (and this is strange and wondrous indeed) that Jesus has needs. So it is with his followers here and now. His continual call is, 'Get up! I need you to . . .'

2

Jesus realizes

———•◆•———

Who do people say that I am?

I think it's something that dawns on you with the most ghastly inexorable sense. I didn't suddenly wake up in my pram one day and say 'Yippee,' you know.[1]

This is the way that the 21-year-old Prince Charles described what it felt like as he came to realize that he was a king in waiting. In the English language 'to realize' has two meanings. It can mean to gain insight or understanding: Prince Charles gradually realized who he was – the heir to the throne. But it can also mean to make something that has potential (an idea, a talent, a seed) become physical, tangible and bear fruit – to actualize. In a constitutional sense at least, Prince Charles' full potential will not be realized until he accedes to the throne, until he becomes the person he was born to be.

Like Prince Charles, Jesus of Nazareth was a man born to be king, and the understanding of his special destiny is something that will have dawned upon him gradually. Like Prince Charles, Jesus had to wrestle with questions about the nature of his kingship. Again like Prince Charles, Jesus was required to make his self-understanding real, but also to wait for the right time[2] before his potential could be fully realized.

In a lesser sense these are psychological tasks that face us all. The big questions in life tend to be organized around the nature of the universe and our place in it, our identity, our self-worth and the right way to live out our lives.[3] That is, we return time and again, especially at periods of difficulty or change such as adolescence and mid-life, to questions of this sort:

- Who am I?
- Am I worth anything?
- Does life have any meaning or purpose, and is this purpose good – is there hope?
- How am I to live the good life?

We don't find answers to such questions on our own. They are negotiated through our encounters and relationships with others, especially 'significant others' – parents, teachers, friends; that is, the answers are constructed in a social context. How did Prince Charles come to know that he was a king in waiting? Quite simply, other people told him so by word and action. Other people behaved with due deference, addressing him as 'Sir' or 'Your Royal Highness' from an early age; other people, especially his beloved grandmother, showed him evidence of his royal heritage, and so on. Prince Charles is clear that the process was a gradual one of making sense, piecing together the evidence and working out the implications, rather than a sudden *eureka* moment. He is also clear that his dawning understanding brought with it a sense of burden. Yet his reference to a joyful 'Yippee!' is an acknowledgement that being heir to the throne is a privilege. So, when you realize that you are the heir to the throne you also gain the assurance that you are very important – you attain a sense of self-worth.

Jesus too came to a clear understanding of his identity and self-worth. It is highly likely that the process was one of gradual awakening, though we can only engage in educated guessing as to what form this awakening took. What seems certain is that the beginning of his public ministry coincided with a special experience of divine assurance and endorsement. Matthew, Mark and Luke tell us that at the time of his baptism Jesus experienced a heavenly vision and heard a voice that assured him both of his identity (the Son of God) and of his worth (beloved of his Father and pleasing to his Father). They indicate that while the watching crowd knew that something significant had happened, part of what took place was for Jesus alone. It is only Jesus who sees 'the heavens open' (Mark 1.10 and parallels). We are told that a voice comes from heaven, but it is not made clear whether the crowd hears what the voice is saying.[4] The message is for Jesus himself. Jesus comes to know who he is because someone else – his 'significant other' – tells him.

There is no doubt that a key characteristic of the man Jesus is that he related to YHWH – the Lord – as his primary significant other. We don't know how this came about. Perhaps Jesus had an embryonic but assured sense of closeness to the Lord from the earliest age, which matured with him as he grew. Or perhaps the young Jesus yearned for something or someone who seemed to be missing in his life, and discovered that this special someone was the Lord. The second alternative is perhaps more psychologically plausible[5] simply because the young Jesus had quite a lot missing in his life. The circumstances of his birth were odd, if not scandalous (Matthew 1.19).[6] He was part of a family, but the head of that family was not his biological father and was certainly out of the picture by the time Jesus was a young adult, if not long before. He came from a rather squalid little village with nothing to recommend it (John 1.46). These things may have fuelled Jesus' search for significance. He had an *aspiration* to a different father, and a different family from the Joseph clan in Nazareth (Mark 3.33–34). He also clearly had a highly developed *awareness* of the immanence of the divine, both in his daily life and in the natural world he inhabited.[7] This combination of aspiration and awareness would have provided the right psychological conditions for Jesus to develop a sense of special filial intimacy with the Lord.

Whatever its childhood origins, Jesus' belief that he was the beloved Son of God must have come about gradually, in a life

19

history that was punctuated by 'self-defining memories'[8] – key events or moments of insight that form the building blocks of our identity. And the Synoptic[9] Gospels paint a picture that suggests that Jesus' identity was a 'work in progress' throughout his life – a dynamic realization – rather than a fixed position, something that literally involved work:

- working out whether he really is God's son
- working out what it means to be God's son
- doing the work of God's son.

What is striking about this work is that according to the gospel writers Jesus did not go about it only through mystical communion with God; he also used some other unusual dialogue partners to help him. Some of these were 'critical friends', others were frank enemies. All were essential players in those self-defining moments that became for him, and later for the Church, sacred self-defining memories.

We have Satan's dialogue with Jesus in the temptation narratives that begins, '*if* you are the Son of God' (Matthew 4.1–11; Luke 4.1–13); the repeated cries of recognition by demonized people (e.g. Mark 1.24);[10] Jesus' strange dependency on the attitude of the people in the synagogue at Nazareth, where he is unable fully to actualize his identity as the Son of God (Mark 6.3–5); and his genuine question to the disciples at Caesarea Philippi, 'But who do *you* say that I am?', which evokes Peter's realization of Jesus' identity (Matthew 16.15–16 and parallels).[11]

So, apart from his primary relationship with the Lord, there seem to have been a lot of 'significant others' in Jesus' life, and most of these were human beings. This should not surprise us if we remember the name that Jesus chose to describe himself was not 'Son of God', but 'Son of Humankind',[12] a term that emphasizes his solidarity with his human brethren, but may also indicate the pre-eminence of the eldest child who looks out for his younger siblings. If Jesus' vision was for a renewed family that had *God* as its patriarchal head, this family was to consist of *human beings* living as brothers and sisters. Later in this chapter we will consider the involvement of two of these sisters, Mary of Nazareth and a Gentile woman, self-defining moments in the life of Jesus.

In the gospel accounts Jesus' identity emerges in the context of interchanges with other human beings, and it is a deeply controversial issue. Sometimes his identity as 'Messiah' and 'Son of God' is confirmed to him by simple statements such as those of Peter and Martha (John 11.27). Sometimes an alternative identity is presented to him, for instance the Pharisees' charge that he is working for or related to Beelzebul (Matthew 12.24; Luke 11.15). But there is more to the controversy than the question of whether Jesus is of God or of the devil. At least as important is the question of what it would *mean* to be of God, what the nature of the work of the Son of God actually is.

This question is the real focus of Matthew's and Luke's accounts of the temptation. (Note how this follows on directly from Jesus' baptism experience in which his identity as God's Son has been confirmed to him.) Here Satan presents Jesus with a picture of what the Son of God is like. He has power over nature, which he can use to meet his own immediate needs; he has power over all the kingdoms of the world to use as he wishes; he is free to exploit the love of God by testing it in whatever way he likes. Peter presents a similar picture when, having named Jesus as the Son of God, he refuses to accept that his identity entails suffering and death (Mark 8.32–33 and parallels). In John's Gospel Jesus has to flee from people who, having identified him as 'the prophet who has come into the world', try to make him king by force (John 6.14–15). All four gospel writers highlight the very real danger of misunderstanding what it means to be the Son of God – what the work of the Son of God really is – by placing insights into Jesus' identity directly alongside travesties of the true meaning of that identity. They make it clear that Jesus himself wrestled with the issue, and that the feedback he received from those around him could either support or undermine him in his quest for true insight with integrity – 'You are a stumbling block to me!'

Jesus was engaged in a quest to work out whether he truly was God's son, to work out what that meant, and then to work at doing it. And the quest seems to have involved more than simple labour; there was challenge and even fighting. The tone of Jesus' interactions with others on this subject is at times tetchy. It carries with it a sense of the frustration and irritation that can go with supremely focused attention and extraordinary mental, physical or spiritual effort.

What am I to you, woman?

The Gospel of Luke tells of an early conversation between Jesus and his mother concerning the issue of his identity (Luke 2.41–51). Jesus is 12 years old, entering the age of adulthood, and has stayed behind in the Temple participating in the teaching that is taking place there, while his parents have already begun the journey back to Galilee. In this account Mary is in the foreground and Joseph is a shadowy figure. This is necessary for the story whose punchline conveys the fact that Jesus' true father is not Joseph at all, but the Lord. Mary has the literary function of providing Jesus with the phrase, '*Your father and I . . .*', which he can counter with, 'I must be in *my Father's* house.' But this story is more than a simple narrative that sets the scene for a final pronouncement, and Mary does more than feed Jesus his line.

The issue of Mary's relationship with Jesus, and the hurt that is entailed in her becoming the Lord's servant, is communicated with some sensitivity by Luke.[13] Mary does not come over to us as a two-dimensional literary device but as a flesh-and-blood mother who is perplexed and wounded by her son's behaviour. This is conveyed by her remark that the search for Jesus has been one of 'great anxiety' (*odunōmenoi*). The same word is used later in the Gospel by Luke to describe the agonizing torment of Dives in the flames of Hades (Luke 16.24). It's an appropriate word to use. Anyone who has lost a child, even for a few moments, will know that the experience is better described by the word 'agony' than 'anxiety'.

The search has been systematic and lengthy, and presumably exhausting. Mary's first words when she sees her son are words of indignant accusation, and an attempt to assert her authority over him with the address 'Child!' (which may also indicate affection). The young Jesus might be expected to apologize or to defend his action. Instead he responds with a simple wrong-footing of his mother as he expresses wonder at his parents' lack of perception that he has bigger fish to fry than the concerns of the Joseph clan.

Jesus is asserting the beginnings of an adult life. In the contemporary Western world we are used to thinking about adulthood as emerging during a fairly leisurely liminal period in the teens and early twenties called 'adolescence'. It would be anachronistic to talk of an 'adolescent' Jesus. Nevertheless, there are features in this story that connect with what Erik Erikson has referred to as the central task of adolescence, that of ego consolidation.[14] Part of this task is the repudiation of alternative egos, the management of 'role confusion'. In order to achieve a sense of adult identity the young psyche must distance itself from competing identities.

Jesus' decision to remain in Jerusalem has already geographically distanced himself from the homeward-bound Joseph clan, and he now states his identity in a way that does not allow for any role confusion: he must be 'about my Father's business' and, as he has just demonstrated, that business is theology not carpentry.

Mary offers Jesus an authority structure, and with it an identity. He is her child, under her authority, and Joseph is his adoptive father, someone who has given him respectability and a family name. The young Jesus sets himself against his mother's perspective. Her statement of the way things are is the occasion for his assertion that they are *not* that way. Mary is a very significant other in Jesus' life, and she provides something for him to kick against, a relationship that is from its earliest days coloured by loss and detachment. As Jesus starts to become actively engaged in discovering his Father and his Father's business he distances himself from his Nazareth family and his mother. This is the nature of spiritual growth. We not only repudiate *alternative* ways of being and seeing, we repudiate *past* ways of being and seeing: we lose our existing selves (Matthew 10.39 and parallels), we are born anew (John 3.3). And this can be painful for those left behind.

In his 1860 painting *The Finding of the Saviour in the Temple* the pre-Raphaelite artist William Holman Hunt depicts the young Jesus pulling away from the hold of Mary and the touch of Joseph. Jesus strains forward, looking straight out of the picture at something that his parents do not see. Hunt filled his pictures with symbol and allegory, and this work is no exception. In the background it is possible to make out another incident in the Temple courts. A lamb is being separated from its mother. The lamb is without blemish (Leviticus 9.3) and is to be sacrificed. Its mother strains after it, a touching image that is full of pathos. It is easy to imagine the bleating of the mother as she calls for her baby amid all the other noises of the Temple.

So, as Jesus' 'true self' emerges there is hurt for those who have loved him from the beginning. The repeated rebirths along the way bring pain just as the first birth brought pain. The ultimate pain for Mary is, of course, borne at the foot of the cross. Yet this ultimate agonizing separation is anticipated by a lot of little torn adhesions along the way, in the form of sharp or dismissive words from her son.

Nevertheless, there is some sort of two-way transaction going on. Mary brings to Jesus a view whose repudiation makes his identity crystal clear. And, despite his challenge to her authority, we are told that Jesus returns with his parents to Galilee and submits himself to them. What's more, Mary has herself become a new person. The experience changes her perspective. It is perhaps the last time that she unthinkingly calls Jesus 'Child'. She doesn't fully understand her experience but she knows that it is significant. She stores up the memory in a secret place, ready to bring it out when the time is ripe.

Judging when the time is ripe is, of course, difficult, and in John's Gospel we are given an indication that Mary may have got it wrong. There is an interchange between Jesus and Mary that occurs at another liminal moment, as Jesus is poised on the brink of his public ministry (John 2.1–12). If anything, there is even more tension than in Luke's account of their interchange in the Temple. Jesus, his disciples and his mother are guests at a wedding. The wine runs out and Mary draws the fact to Jesus' attention. This time it is Jesus who uses a term of address that might be affectionate, but has the effect of asserting his authority. He calls Mary 'Woman!', and he employs an idiom that asserts a profound distance: *ti emoi kai soi*, literally translated, 'what to me and you?' These are the words shouted at Jesus by the demonized man of Gerasa, immediately after he has identified him as the 'Son of God' (Mark 5.7; Luke 8.28). It is as if Mary at Cana, like Simon Peter at Caesarea Philippi, has for a moment taken on the role of Satan the tempter. For she is presenting Jesus with a situation in which he might use his power simply for convenience, and at a time when he is not yet ready to act. She is, in his view, profoundly out of step with him.

So it is somewhat surprising that Jesus then acts, to all appearances, in accordance with her wishes. It is almost as if what he does is against his better judgement. Mary nudges, prompts (perhaps even nags?[15]) him forward. She is also a key player in what happens next, acting as an authoritative intermediary between Jesus and the servants. There seems to be a deep process of discernment at work here. When Satan suggests to Jesus that he turn stones to bread he is sent packing. When Simon Peter insists that the Messiah must not suffer he is dealt with very sharply. Yet when Mary says, 'They have no wine', Jesus initially resists but then comes round, and as he does this something of his identity is realized. That is why, in the title of this section, I have translated his remark to his mother as, 'What am I to you?'

John tells us that the miracle at the wedding at Cana is the first sign through which Jesus' glory is revealed (John 2.11). It gives him credibility with his followers. This revelation of Jesus' glory, of his identity, to his followers and to himself, happens in response to his mother's faith in him. The time turns out to be right for a foretaste of the glory that will only be fully revealed at the cross.

The turning of water into wine is programmatic for Jesus' whole ministry, for it is a miracle that is all about transformation. It is about the breathing of unimaginable new life into the Jewish law within which Jesus had grown up. The jars that hold the water are ritual purification jars. Jesus is taking his cultural and religious origins and transforming them into something better, different-yet-connected to what they were before. And alongside this there is a transformation of the relationship with his mother, his personal origin, into something different-yet-connected to what it has been before. Something that in the end is better although, as we have seen, at great personal cost.

Scavenging dogs and other sheep

Jesus was the son of Mary of Nazareth and a member of the family of Joseph the carpenter. But, as we have just been reminded, at a more fundamental level he was a Jew. Jesus was circumcised (Luke 2.21); the god he worshipped was the Lord – YHWH – the god of the Jews; he regularly attended the synagogue (Luke 4.16); he kept the Jewish festivals (John 5.1; 7.10); he meditated on the Hebrew Scriptures, and seems to have used rabbinic forms of argument in his teaching. It is in this context that Jesus had to work out what being the Son of God means, and then to do it.

At two points in the Gospels we are told that Jesus 'was amazed by' or 'wondered at' something. He encounters something unexpected, or at least counterintuitive, and responds accordingly. The first occasion for wondering is the cynicism and suspicion with which he is greeted in his home synagogue (Mark 6.6). The second occasion for wondering is the extraordinary faith shown by the centurion who reasons that Jesus can heal his servant at a distance (Matthew 8.10; Luke 7.9). Those who are ethnically, socially and religiously close to Jesus reject him, and a man who is distant in all these respects believes in him. How surprising!

These facts are, of course, only surprising if one's starting assumption is that the mission of the Son of God is inherently a mission to the *people of God*, the mission of the great Good Shepherd to 'seek and save the lost' sheep *of Israel*.

The gospel writers, in particular Matthew, indeed present this as Jesus' starting assumption (Matthew 10.6, 23; 19.28; Mark 10.42–43; Luke 19.9–10; 22.25–26, 30), and it seems to have persisted as a dominant part of his agenda. We can infer this from the fact that the very first Christians, drawn from the ranks of those who had followed him during his lifetime, seem to have conceived of the gospel as good news for *Jews* (understood broadly to include Diaspora Jews, Gentile converts to Judaism, and possibly Samaritans)[16] rather than as good news for the whole world (Acts 11.1). Jesus was a Jew, and the goal of his mission was not Rome – the centre of the world – but Jerusalem, the holy mountain of his own people (Luke 13.33).

Yet the Gospels tell us that right from the beginning of his ministry to his people there was a series of conflicts and outright rejections, especially from those with a claim to be holy or religiously privileged – the scribes, Pharisees and Sadducees. Jesus' welcome for 'sinners'[17] on the margins of Jewish society arose through his primary concern for them, but it is also true

that most of the Jewish elite did not want to be welcomed by
him anyway (Matthew 22.8–9; Luke 14.16–24). The Gospels
tell us that Jesus' response to the regular rejection his ministry
seems to have evoked was to curse the towns and villages that
would not receive him. In his grief, frustration and perplexity
he compares Jewish towns like Capernaum unfavourably with
Gentile towns like Tyre and Sidon, and talks of the *Gentile*
Queen of Sheba rising up in judgement against sceptical Jews
who demand a sign (Matthew 12.42; Luke 11.31). Finally he
weeps bitter and poignant tears over Jerusalem. And behind
the cursing and weeping lies a question. If the work of the Son
of God is to reach out and bring home the morally and geographically lost people of Israel, why do so few want to be
helped?

Jesus' thinking must have been deeply influenced by his
knowledge of the Hebrew Scriptures. As he went about Galilee
proclaiming that the time is fulfilled and the kingdom of God
is drawing near, he must have had in mind many images of
the Day of the Lord drawn from the prophets and psalms.[18]
These are images of terrible judgement against oppressors
within Israel and without; of vindication of a morally pure
remnant of God's people; of the coming home of those scattered far afield by invading nations. But also among these
images are little glimpses of *other* nations who finally understand that the Lord is the one true God. These nations come
in humiliation to bring tribute (Isaiah 45.14), with eagerness
to ask for instruction (Isaiah 2.3), even to be joined to God's
people (Zechariah 2.11).

These glimpses in the Scriptures offered Jesus some conceptual space for the Gentiles in the kingdom of God, as a
background to his mission that was naturally focused on the
Jews. As he experienced rejection by Jews and odd instances
of Gentile acceptance, the inhabitants of this conceptual space
may have started to move to the foreground of his consciousness: 'I tell you, many will come from east and west and will eat

with Abraham and Isaac and Jacob in the kingdom of heaven' (Matthew 8.11; see also Luke 13.29).

As Jesus' horizon broadened his identity became more fully realized, and the nature of his work became clearer. Two of the gospel writers focus this broadening of horizon on a difficult encounter with a 'critical friend' – a Gentile woman (Matthew 15.21–28; Mark 7.24–30).

This is a story that you wouldn't make up if your intention were to present Jesus in a good light. A desperate foreign woman comes to him for help on behalf of a tormented child. He refuses, calling her a dog in the process. She persists, turning his words to her advantage by claiming that even dogs are entitled to leftovers, and he relents and grants her request. On this occasion Jesus comes over as cold (especially in Matthew's version in which he at first ignores the woman's entreaties), unkind, outsmarted, and of changeable mind. On the other hand, if you believe that Jesus was always warm, universally caring, omniscient and immutable of purpose, you will tend to see in the texts signs of all of these. Is he perhaps joking with the woman in order to comfort her (after all, he calls her a 'little' dog)? Is he perhaps testing the woman's faith in order to strengthen her? Has he intended to heal her daughter right from the start? Does he permit her to make her point in order to enlighten the observers? And so on.

Matthew and Mark provide no evidence at all in favour of such conjectures. Indeed they do not seem to have been bothered that readers throughout the centuries might find this story unpalatable. Palatability was not part of their agenda; their job was to pass on the Jesus tradition received from eyewitnesses.[19] The very unpleasantness of the story is a sign of the respect that the gospel writers had for the material entrusted to them, and a strong indicator that it refers to a real historical incident. The woman's metaphor of dogs eating leftover breadcrumbs under a table is both apt and easy to visualize. This will have assured the widespread transmission[20] of the story in the first Christian communities. It is likely that there were several oral versions, all with the same gist, and all containing that memorable canine metaphor.

The incident seems to have occurred in the region of Tyre and Sidon. This is hugely significant for, as we have seen, Jesus compared these ancient Phoenician towns favourably with the Galilean towns that had rejected him (Matthew 11.20–22; Luke 10.13–14). However, this isn't so much a compliment to Tyre and Sidon as it is an insult to the Galilean towns. It is rather like saying about one's new boss, 'He makes Hitler seem cuddly.' For Tyre and Sidon were not simply neutral Gentile towns. They were in a northwestern region that had for many hundreds of years formed a kind of buffer between ancient Israel and those who wished to contaminate her culture or to invade and destroy her. If trouble came, it came from the north or west, and it often came via the sea ports of Tyre and Sidon. Indeed the cargo traded through these ports may once have included Israelite slaves captured on raids inland (see, for instance, Amos 1.9–10). When Jesus travelled to this region he was very clearly entering *enemy* territory. (This may lead us to wonder why he went there at all, and I will return to this question shortly.)

Talk of enemies is common in the Hebrew Scriptures, and nowhere more common than in the psalms.[21] The psalms were the hymns of ancient Israel, and for ordinary Jews at the time of Jesus they would have been like religious wallpaper, so deeply familiar that they were taken for granted. In the psalms enemies are hated, but more often enemies are feared. The psalmist repeatedly expresses feelings of being surrounded by those who desire his destruction, pressing in on him from all sides. To the modern reader this can sound like the cries of a person who feels at the mercy of dark emotional or spiritual forces, or else in danger from compatriots who have turned against him. (It is always 'him' because the psalms are male compositions.)[22] However, the psalmist may often be speaking for all the people, and in this case the enemies represent other nations pressing in from the north and the west, whose minds are firmly set on the destruction of Israel. The enemies are described as dangerous animals, sometimes as 'dogs': 'For dogs are all around me; a company of evildoers encircles me' (Psalm 22.16, NRSV).

These are not winsome house pets or faithful working dogs but more like savage pit bulls capable of killing and eating their victim. To be eaten by dogs (the ultimate fate of many crucifixion victims) was the most shameful end to a life imaginable. After all, the infamous Queen Jezebel met her end in this way (2 Kings 9.33–37).

Psalm 59 expands the canine imagery, describing the dogs as 'prowling' and significantly 'crying aloud', often translated as 'howling'.[23] The howling is spine-chilling and full of threat. So it is interesting that Matthew, never one to waste words, labours the point that the Gentile woman who approaches Jesus on northwestern enemy territory is *ekrazen* – calling out or shouting.

From the perspective of Jesus, the single rural Jew, this woman is entirely 'other'. She is a Gentile urban dweller, probably wealthy, perhaps married but certainly able to operate independently, and with at least one child. What's more Jesus is on her territory. In this respect the encounter is radically different from his meeting with a God-fearing centurion in Semitic administered Capernaum.[24] Humanly speaking, Jesus is way out of his comfort zone. Matthew and Mark tell us that he has withdrawn to this uncomfortable (and unclean) location following a nasty dispute with the Pharisees about his attitude to some of the purity requirements of the Jewish law, which ends in his making a public pronouncement that directly contradicts received tradition (Matthew 15.10–11; Mark 7.14–15). Jesus has been pressing at the boundaries of the law in the places where mindless conformity or conscious abuse gets in the way of true holiness. In doing this he moves into a new and perhaps disquieting theological place, and then finds himself travelling to a strange and definitely disquieting geographical location where a howling woman presses upon him. At several levels he is treading on dangerous ground, and it is perhaps not surprising that he seems to have dogs on his mind.

Mark makes the surely historically accurate observation that the woman was a Syro-Phoenician, in other words a native of the area. In contrast, Matthew says something extraordinary about her. He describes her as a 'Canaanite'. This term fell out of use many centuries before the time of Jesus, so it is akin to a twenty-first-century Briton describing a north African as a 'Moor' or a Dane as a 'Viking'. In using the strange term 'Canaanite' Matthew seems to be making another connection with Queen Jezebel, who was herself a Phoenician and a daughter of the king of Tyre. The name Jezebel was and still is today a byword for treachery, for she engineered the killing of Naboth for simple monetary gain (1 Kings 21.1–16). But this is merely secondary to a more fundamental crime – the enticement of her Israelite husband King Ahab to worship the Baals of the Canaanite cult (1 Kings 16.30–33).

Much of the history of the people of God as set out in the Hebrew Scriptures is one of radical separation from the vegetative nature religions of the peoples who lived alongside them, collectively referred to as Canaanites. The degree of hostility expressed to these religions by the biblical patriarchs and prophets is marked, and from time to time expressed in acts of great physical violence, the most shocking of which is the massacre of the prophets of Baal by Jehu recounted in 2 Kings 10. The kings of Israel and Judah are judged by the biblical historians in terms of their degree of resistance to or collusion with the Baal cults. These cults offered sacrifices on raised platforms called 'high places' adorned with poles in honour of the goddess Ashera. Jewish resistance to these local religious practices is seen by the biblical writers as desirable because it indicates faithfulness to the Lord's covenant with David (2 Samuel 7), and with Moses before him. Collusion with these practices is seen as adulterous apostasy, as simply asking for divine punishment. After all, God had spoken:

> Take care not to make a covenant with the inhabitants of the
> land to which you are going, or it will become a snare among
> you. You shall tear down their altars, break their pillars, and cut
> down their sacred poles (for you shall worship no other god,
> because the LORD, whose name is Jealous, is a jealous God).
>
> (Exodus 34.12–14, NRSV)

An enlightening perspective on the hostilities between ancient Judaism and the religion of the Canaanites is offered by the psychologist Ian Suttie in a fascinating book published in 1935 entitled *The Origins of Love and Hate*.[25] His work is an example of 'psychology of religion', a discipline that approaches religion as a human response to transcendent aspects of the universe. The aim is not to explain God away, but to understand better the patterns of behaviour that people throughout history have shown when they think that they are dealing with God. God through his grace may inhabit, transfigure and reveal himself through religion, but religion will always have a human psychological component that can repay study in its own right.

Suttie argued that disturbing aspects of early parental relationships, particularly jealousy, are played out, managed and become institutionalized in adult religion. On the basis of ethnographic studies he identified two sharply contrasting types of religion: cults of father-gods and cults of mother-goddesses. Father-god cults, which are typical of patriarchal societies, are characterized by two sorts of jealousy: the male's jealousy of the female's capacity to reproduce,[26] and the son's jealousy of his father.[27] These jealousies are managed by animal blood sacrificial rites that mimic the blood of childbearing, but from which women are always excluded. These sacrifices seem to play a key part in confirming paternity and thus a son's inheritance rights. They also maintain the authority of the father over his sons, who are required to obey his cultic and moral strictures.

According to Suttie, in mother-goddess cults, more typical of matrifocal societies, the jealousy is that of siblings in competition for the nurture of their mother. As mother-goddesses tend to be associated with the earth, sacrifices in these sorts of cults are the fruits of the earth – vegetables, cereals, or cooked meats. (A key difference from the father-god cults is that blood is not of itself important.) However, from time to time, human – often infant – sacrifices may be required. The suggestion is that such sacrifices enact the supplanting of an existing child by a new sibling with whom worshippers can identify, and thus manage their own sibling jealousy.

Suttie argued that early Israelite religion had aspects of both father-god and mother-goddess cults, and he used the story of Cain and Abel in Genesis 3 to explore the tensions between the two. However, there is no doubt that as the Israelite nation developed it went very much in Suttie's father-god direction. Its religious and national identity was expressed and confirmed through cultic animal blood sacrifice, a patriarchal social structure with an emphasis on descendants who could be traced back to a named father, a high moral code that emphasized obedience and respect for paternal authority, a marginalization of women, and a horror of human sacrifice. (Genesis 22 seems to sum much of this up.) Not only that, its professed aim was to stamp out anything associated with mother-goddess religions such as the ancient Canaanite cults, which were seen as profound threats to its fundamental and distinctive identity.

The religion that Jesus inherited, and within which he encountered the living God, was overwhelmingly patriarchal[28] and sternly set against its surrounding culture, including the strongly feminine aspects of that culture's religious heritage.

The fact that the Syro-Phoenician who comes to Jesus is a woman is therefore crucial, and we can now see that their difference goes beyond a surface difference of gender between two individuals. She stands for all that lies outside and is at odds with Jesus' patriarchal culture, for all that has for centuries been avoided and hated as godless by his people, for all that they have defined themselves against. She stands for idolatry, for polytheism, for child sacrifice, for apostasy. In the assertiveness of her request she stands for the strident and dominant Queen Jezebel who dared to set herself against the *man* of God, Elijah. What's more, her concern is maternal, if not frankly matriarchal, with strong hints of uncontrolled reproductive power. She is an independent female asking for help for her female offspring.

Jesus' reaction is to reiterate the focus of his mission to his own people, emphasizing that there is something 'improper' about including others, especially one so profoundly 'other', within its scope. It's hard to see what else he could do as a faithful Jew, for – to stay with the bread metaphor – he is being asked to consider something equivalent to eating a bacon sandwich.

The woman, probably driven by desperation, then does something extremely clever. She doesn't argue with Jesus' description of her and her family. Instead she accepts the insulting image and transforms it, offering it back so that, while remaining an insult, it can work in her favour. And now, perhaps because transformation is Jesus' stock in trade, there is a connection between them. On his part there is surprise, maybe a smile, certainly respect. And finally there is *realization* – for Jesus heals her daughter. Jesus does this despite himself or, more correctly, despite the Jesus he used to be until he met this woman.

How strange it is that Jesus seems to need to have an encounter with this woman in order to realize that there are other sheep that must be brought in (John 10.16)! How strange that she seems to offer him something that he doesn't already have, and has not until now consciously realized that he needs.

This feels like the stuff of romantic love. It's certainly the stuff of Lizzy Bennet and Mr Darcy, a man who is intent on avoiding her and her noisy, troublesome family at all costs because they seem – indeed are – beneath him, but who finds he cannot truly be himself without what she brings to him:

> 'I was almost taught . . . to care for none beyond my family circle, to think meanly of all the rest of the world . . . and such might still have been but for you, dearest, loveliest Elizabeth! What do I not owe you? You taught me a lesson, hard at first, but most advantageous.'

Of course, this quote is playful on my part, and any hints of passion or romance in the story of Jesus and the Syro-Phoenician woman are the projections of those of us with a fondness for romantic heroes. But this story of an outsider who can establish a brief intimacy with Jesus has a certain frisson, and there is no doubt that the woman, like Lizzy Bennet, is raised up by the experience. Her daughter is healed; her clever words go down in history; above all, she has the privilege of playing a part in Jesus' developing understanding of his mission. Matthew and Mark make this very clear by the way they place this encounter in their Gospels.

As we have seen, the story of the Syro-Phoenician woman follows Jesus' dispute with the Pharisees about what it is that makes a person pure, culminating in his conclusion that motivation is more important than outward religious forms. She is an extreme and therefore salient example of this point, a ritually unclean person who comes to Jesus in hope and faith. Shortly before his dispute with the Pharisees Jesus has fed 5,000 people with bread and fish. There are 12 baskets of food left over, signifying the 12 tribes of Israel. Immediately after his meeting with the woman, Jesus goes on to feed 4,000 more people who, according to Matthew, 'glorified the God of Israel' (Matthew 15.31), thus implying that they are in some sense outsiders. There are seven baskets of food left over, which may be taken to signify the completeness of Jesus' mission to the whole world.

It can be seen that Matthew and Mark have chosen to locate the story of the Syro-Phoenician woman at the point where a mission that is focused on the Jews becomes a mission that spreads out from this focus to include the whole world. They take the psychology of this encounter between Jesus and 'the other' and give it a central position in Jesus' theological journey. The woman's cry of 'Me too!' also anticipates Paul's assertion in his letter to the Romans that the good news of Jesus Christ is for the Jew first and then for the Greek (Romans 1.16; 2.9–10).

Somewhere along the way, however, the Jesus I mentioned earlier in this chapter – the one who is always warm, polite, universally caring, omniscient and of immutable purpose – has disappeared. And this is surely right, for such a Jesus is less than human. He has been replaced by the Jesus we have seen arguing with two critical friends – his beloved mother and a foreign stranger. This Jesus is instead abrasive, flexible, dynamic, potent, developing yet always on-task. He is a proper and worthy Son of Humankind. But the astonishingly radical transformation that we see at work in him during his conversations with these women, the transformation that spreads like a fire further than even he had at first envisaged, helps us to realize something else. It is this: Jesus heard aright the voice that told him, 'You are *my* Son, the Beloved; with you I am well pleased.'

3

Jesus saves

Such women

Then Jesus went to the Mount of Olives. And early in the morning he again appeared in the temple. All the people were coming to him, and having taken his seat he was teaching them. The scribes and the Pharisees bring in a woman caught in adultery, and having placed her in the middle, they say to him, 'Teacher, this woman was caught in the act of being seduced. In our law Moses commanded such women to be stoned. So, what do *you* say?' Now they said this to test him, in order that they might get something with which to accuse him. But Jesus, having stooped down, was tracing with his finger in the earth.   (John 8.1–6)

The story of the woman taken in adultery is a story of salvation, perhaps *the* story of salvation in the New Testament, for it is a story that offers an account both of what we are saved from and of how Jesus saves. In the previous chapter we considered the way in which Jesus' identity as Son of Humankind and Son of God was made real through encounters and negotiations with others. The issue of Jesus' identity continues to be important in this chapter. I argue that Jesus' response to the situation of the woman taken in adultery flows out of his personal and family history. The nature of his saving act is a manifestation of who he is.

The story is of very ancient provenance.[1] Like the story of the Gentile woman, it is striking and memorable, and there is probably a long oral tradition behind it. However, it is absent from the majority of early gospel manuscripts, and it is placed in varying locations in the ones where it does appear. Most manuscripts that do have it place it at some point in John's Gospel, but some place it in Luke's Gospel, and the style suggests that Luke was the author. The fifth-century Codex Bezae[2] places it following John 7.52, where we find it in most modern versions.

Codex Bezae is interesting because it has some additional unique material. This includes a pronouncement by Jesus on seeing a man working on the Sabbath, placed following Luke 6.4.[3] The Mosaic law prescribed stoning as a punishment for working on the Sabbath, and there is an account of such a stoning in Numbers 15. Gender pairings are common in the teaching of Jesus, as we shall see in Chapter 7. So, perhaps we have a gender pair preserved in Codex Bezae; Jesus' responses to a man and a woman who each, under the letter of the law, merit death by stoning.

In his book *The God Delusion* Richard Dawkins refers to the divinely sanctioned practice of stoning Sabbath-breakers as an argument for the immorality of God.[4] It is easy to see where he is coming from. However you look at it, the practice is cruel and barbaric. What Dawkins doesn't acknowledge, perhaps through ignorance or perhaps because it doesn't suit his polemical purpose in that book, is the complexity of attitudes to the issue within Judaism over the centuries. And of course he ignores Jesus' encounter with the woman taken in adultery and her accusers.

It's important to read this story carefully if one is to make sense of it. The question presented to Jesus is not, 'Shall we stone her now?' but a more hypothetical problem in which the woman is used as an illustration. One reason for this may be that by about AD 30 the death penalty for violations of the Jewish law could not be enacted except through appeal to the Roman administration, which was very unlikely to grant such a suit.[5] (There is an obvious similarity here to the charges of blasphemy brought against Jesus, to which we shall return.)

We are told that the woman's accusers have set up the case in order to entrap Jesus in some way. It must therefore place him in a catch-22 situation. Yet, on the face of it, there is no dilemma for him to address. The law is clear. The woman has been caught in the act, presumably by the two required witnesses (Deuteronomy 17.6). It should be a simple open-and-shut case. This seems to be confirmed by Jesus, for he calls neither the woman's guilt nor the legal procedures employed into question. Yet her accusers have come, as if perplexed, to seek his expert opinion as he sits teaching in the Temple. So, where is the dilemma?

It is the same dilemma faced by us today, and highlighted by Richard Dawkins: for most civilized people stoning a woman to death for sexual misconduct (whether or not she was a 'consenting' participant) feels draconian, to say the least. There is evidence that at the time of Jesus, thoughtful Jews also had such scruples, and it is likely that local flexibility and discretion were exercised in the application of the Mosaic law in many areas of life.[6] The question that is being put to Jesus is therefore this: 'If we show mercy to this woman, as many might be inclined to do, are we not calling the sovereignty and justice of God into question?'

This is not a dilemma for Dawkins because God doesn't come into the equation for him: stoning the woman would be irrational and despicable. Neither is it a dilemma for those of a religious fundamentalist mindset whose desire to 'honour' God rides roughshod over human compassion: stoning the woman would be a moral obligation. Neither is it a dilemma for those of sadistic temperament who get enjoyment, including sexual gratification, from hurting and humiliating others, especially the weak and vulnerable: stoning the woman would be fun.

But it *is* a dilemma for a man who is renowned both for his extremely strict teaching on marriage and divorce (Matthew 19.1–12), and his compassionate attitude to individuals who have sinned (Matthew 9.11 and parallels). If Jesus makes a pronouncement that is weighted too much in the direction of compassion he can be accused of teaching disregard for the divinely appointed law. His enemies will have 'something with which to accuse him'. If he makes a pronouncement in line with the letter of the law, he gives the lie to his message of the liberating good news of God's kingdom (Matthew 4.23 and parallels).

Yet there is more going on here than a tension between mercy and justice. There are the questions of Jesus' own origins, and the mysterious circumstances of his conception.[7] If Jesus agrees that *this* woman should be stoned he in some sense condemns all 'such women'. In so doing he condemns his own mother, stigmatizes himself, and again plays into the hands of his enemies.

Jesus' origins are the cause of a number of derogatory comments in the New Testament. 'Can anything good come out of Nazareth?' asks Nathanael when he first hears about Jesus (John 1.46, NRSV). Later in John's Gospel, a group of Judaeans ask Jesus, 'Are we not right in saying that you are a Samaritan and have a demon?' (John 8.48, NRSV). Most telling of all is Joseph's reaction on discovering that his young wife[8] is pregnant. Matthew tells us that because Joseph was a man of personal integrity he decided to break his betrothal to Mary privately by quietly divorcing her. This would have been an attractive option to a woman in her position because the alternative was a public enquiry which could have culminated in her stoning.[9] So, in planning to treat Mary's presumed adultery[10] as a private matter, Joseph was effectively saving her life. Matthew tells us that Joseph then changed his mind as the result of divine revelation, and kept Mary and her child under his protection. But others were not privy to Joseph's experience. There must have been gossip, and people would have drawn their own conclusions. Well into the second century at least, one opponent of Christianity was claiming that Jesus was illegitimate and his mother a prime example of 'such women'.[11]

So, Mary of Nazareth was perhaps always under suspicion. It is impossible that Jesus' thoughts did not turn to his mother as the woman taken in adultery was brought to him. However, both Mary and Jesus had been under the protection of a respectable man, and by association they benefited from his probity. Any possible shame or stigma had been covered by the virtue of Joseph who, we are told, was of royal blood – a direct descendant of King David. Joseph had 'made an honest woman' of Mary.

Yet, if we look more closely at Joseph's background we find that this too seems questionable. Right at the beginning of his Gospel Matthew sets out a detailed genealogy for Joseph which goes back 42 generations to Abraham. Genealogies are important for they establish identity. In a patrilineal society identity is conferred by connection with a named biological father; in a matrilineal society it is conferred by connection with a maternal uncle. Women do not have a role in genealogies.

Matthew's and Luke's versions of Joseph's genealogy differ from each other at several points. For instance, Matthew emphasizes Abraham, the father of the Jews, while Luke goes right back to Adam, the father of mankind. But they are both patrilineages whose basic function is to confirm Joseph's descent from King David. On this they agree. The point they are making is the point made by Paul when he describes Jesus as: 'descended from David according to the flesh and . . . declared to be Son of God with power according to the spirit of holiness by resurrection from the dead' (Romans 1.3b–4, NRSV).

For Matthew, Luke and Paul, Jesus' human identity is conferred by Joseph, not Mary. Joseph's identity is conferred by a line of fathers stretching back to the first patriarch. This is a discourse that is all about males. Furthermore, the fact that Matthew places a patrilineage right at the start of his Gospel should not surprise us, for Matthew stands out among the gospel writers as the most androcentric.[12] He is starting his Gospel as he means to continue – writing from the perspective of men. It is then especially striking that four women – Tamar, Rahab, Ruth and Bathsheba – find their way into his genealogy.

These four women are the carriers of Jesus' ancestors. They do not confer blood lineage, they are merely the wombs that house the growing seeds of his progenitors. For the purposes of the genealogy they do not need to be mentioned at all. They do not have conventional honour[13] or ethnic purity to recommend them. None of them is a virgin bride and none of them is Jewish. Indeed their stories are, to varying extents, murky. Yet here they are.

Tamar (Genesis 38.6–30) was a resourceful Canaanite who had married into the tribe of Judah, was widowed, and then neglected by her husband's family. Her child Perez was conceived as a result of her father-in-law impregnating her under the mistaken impression that she was a temple prostitute. By tricking him in this way Tamar secured for herself the place in the family that he had previously denied her. Rahab (Joshua 2 and 6) was a Canaanite secular prostitute who secured the safety of her household amid the destruction of Jericho by helping Joshua's spies. Ruth was a Moabite widow who kept her mother-in-law and herself from starvation by offering herself to her dead husband's kinsman Boaz (Ruth 3.9). Bathsheba, a Hittite, was also a survivor. At any rate she outlasted her husband, Uriah (2 Samuel 11), and came willingly or unwillingly to be the mistress and then wife of King David.

These foreign women, like Austen's Charlotte Lucas, essentially did what they had to do in a man's world when they were faced with situations that offered few options for survival. In this sense they are unremarkable. Yet each seems to have brought something positive to the people of God. The house of Perez, Tamar's son, grew strong and earned high repute (Ruth 4.12). Rahab enabled the Israelites to enter the promised land, and was welcomed into its people, achieving a matriarch-like status by the time of Jesus (Hebrews 11.31; James 2.25;

Josephus, *Antiquities*, 5.1). Bathsheba's son Solomon is described as especially beloved of God (2 Samuel 12.24).

It is Ruth alone who is portrayed as having had some sort of
choice in her life. As a new widow she was given the option
of returning to her people and finding a new husband from
among them. In this context her words to her Jewish mother-
in-law are highly enlightening: 'Where you go, I will go; where
you lodge, I will lodge; your people shall be my people, and
your God my God' (Ruth 1.16, NRSV).

Ruth speaks for all these women, potential bearers of foreign
pollution who instead bring blessing to the nation of Israel.
All are characterized by a turning from their origins and an
embrace of the Jewish God. Like the 'Canaanite' woman, in
desperate situations they are drawn to the Lord and receive
a welcome. Like Mary,[14] their positions are ambiguous, but
their situations are transformed and they are raised up by
God. These liminal, ambiguous women are not only part of
Jesus' family line, they are part of the national heritage. This
is Matthew's point. The drawing of 'all nations' (Matthew
28.19) to the Church, the drawing of the 'other' towards Christ
is anticipated by the coming of the Magi to adore the young
Jesus; it is, as we have seen, anticipated by the faith of the
'Canaanite' woman; and it is anticipated by these foreign
women in the royal lineage. That's why Matthew reminds us
about them.

From the perspective of the Jewish nation these four women
are examples of incomers who have found a place among God's
people; on this view the good end justifies the means used to
achieve it, even if sexual misconduct has been involved. This
contrasts with the position of a woman who is already one of
Israel's 'own' and is thought to have engaged in sexual misconduct. She is a woman who should be under the authority
of her family but who has become out of control, and threatens
to bring disorder, chaos and shame upon her clan. She must
be dealt with.

The case of Tamar[15] is interesting because she found herself in both positions; Tamar was an incomer who then got out of control. She was a foreigner who was chosen and therefore welcomed as a wife for Er, the eldest son of Judah. She married into the tribe of Judah and was placed under his authority. Her husband died, and we are told that this was because he was displeasing to the Lord. So, as was the custom, his younger brother Onan married Tamar. But, because he knew that any children she bore him would be designated sons of Er, he adopted the contraceptive method of *coitus interruptus.* This also displeased the Lord and Onan too died. Judah drew what to him was an obvious conclusion: there must be something wrong with *Tamar.* He didn't want his remaining sons to die through contamination by her, so he sent her back to her father's home to live as a widow. In this way he neglected his duty to her. Later Judah discovers that Tamar is pregnant, and is told that she has been involved in prostitution. (The twist in the story is that she is pregnant by Judah himself, who was quite happy to use her as a prostitute when he didn't know her true identity.)

Even though Tamar is under the care of her father, she is still a member of Judah's tribe. She has brought shame upon it. Unaware that he is the father of the child she is carrying, Judah's reaction is simple: 'Bring her out, and let her be burned' (Genesis 38.24b, NRSV).

In cultures that place a heavy emphasis on honour and shame there is often an unwritten masculine code that requires an honourable man on the one hand to control his own women's virginity and chastity, and on the other hand to exert control over weaker men by taking their women.[16] Losing a woman in an uncontrolled way is thus a mark of masculine weakness, and brings shame on the whole family unit, whose identity and worth is closely linked to that of the leading male. The shame taints the whole family, but its focus is the woman who has been taken. She has also been physically polluted by sexual contact with an unapproved male. So her shame is contagious. The literal contagion that the woman carries is one reason why the method used to dispose of her may necessitate the destruction of her body, for instance by burning, or avoidance of physical contact, for instance by stoning. While this notion of honour-shame cannot be applied wholesale or in a simplistic way to the society of ancient Israel, there is no doubt that some aspects of its life were coloured by it.

Shame can be found to varying extents in most, if not all, human cultures. It is a complex phenomenon that can be understood as part of a social control system – 'shaming people into action' – but also as a painful type of personal distress – 'I felt so ashamed.' Feelings of shame focus on falling short of being the person we aspire to be, and they also have a public dimension. The psychologist Paul Gilbert puts it this way:

> Shame is related to the belief that we cannot create positive images in the eyes of others; we will not be chosen, will be found lacking in talent, ability, appearance and so forth; we will be passed over, ignored, or actively rejected . . . More negatively we may even be the *object* of scorn, contempt, or ridicule to others. We have been disgraced; judged and found wanting in some way.[17]

This is why shame and stigma are so closely related. A stigma is a visible mark that calls a potentially shameful identity to people's attention. When we are ashamed our instinct is to remove ourselves from the public gaze. We manage feelings of shame by hiding or covering stigma, and we fear exposure.

The values of a particular society determine what actually constitutes shame and its stigmata in a given situation. For some magazine editors and readers in the 'civilized' West, cellulite on a female celebrity's thighs would constitute a stigma that the celebrity would do well to hide in shame. (This may seem a trivial example, but it should be remembered that the stigmatizing public gaze has the capacity literally to destroy these celebrities.)

A family or community may choose to cover the focus of its shame, or it may choose to expose it to the public gaze and lance it like a boil. The rationale for the latter is that while this may be painful, the outcome is a removal of a source of infection that could contaminate the whole body. It is a kind of purging.[18] As I have already noted, the punishment for a woman convicted of adultery at the time of Jesus always involved public exposure of her body. In this instance dealing with the community's shame seems to have entailed an unrelenting gaze on the identified focus of that shame.

The woman taken in adultery is brought to Jesus and 'placed in the middle' for all to see. She is the focus of an interesting male debate about justice, but she is also the focus of an important community act of shaming.[19]

All eyes are upon the woman. All, that is, except the eyes of Jesus. Despite an invitation to look at 'this woman' Jesus keeps his eyes fixed on the ground, and in so doing he averts his gaze from her exposed body. His first response is to decline the invitation to participate in her shaming.

The woman stands alone and unprotected, partly or completely naked, abandoned or betrayed by her partner. She is silent before her accusers, who seem to desire a death penalty that they cannot enact without the help of their Roman overlords. Jesus is thus confronted with a human being who evokes both memories and prescience. As surely as he remembers his mother, he also foresees his own fate. The connections between Jesus and this woman are so strong that they approach an *identification* of the one with the other. We have seen that there are resonances with Jesus' ancestry through the line of David, and there are resonances with his personal history in the dangerous circumstances of his conception and birth. We now see that there are resonances with his destiny, centred as it is on abandonment, betrayal, naked exposure to the public gaze, stigma and shame.

Perhaps Jesus averts his eyes from this woman not only to distance himself from her accusers, but also because to gaze on her would be almost unbearably painful. Perhaps he keeps silence not only because he is wisely considering his response, but also because he feels her pain and is nearly crushed by it.

There is a pause. When Jesus finally speaks, there is no doubt that his response saves the situation. But who is saved? And what are they saved from?

You are to name him Jesus, for he will save his people from their sins

Yet they were keeping on asking him and, having straightened up, he said to them, 'He among you who is without sin – let him throw the first stone at her.' And again he stooped down and continued to trace in the earth. But on hearing this, they went out one by one beginning with the eldest, and he was left alone – and also the woman remaining in the middle. Then, having straightened up, Jesus said to her, 'Woman, where are they? Did no one condemn you?' And she said, 'No one, Sir.' Jesus said, 'Neither do I condemn you. Get on with your life, and from now on sin no more.'   (John 8.7–11)

The community wishes to keep itself pure and wholesome – that is, holy.[20] As we have seen, a plausible way that this may be achieved is by exposing and expelling sources of moral pollution that might otherwise infect the whole – lancing the boil. But what if the boil is not a local *source* of infection but a *symptom* of an infection that already inhabits the whole body? (The medical term for this type of infection is 'systemic'.) What if the focus of this community's shame – the woman taken in adultery – is not the source of its problem? What if the individual singled out for blame is not the unique carrier of guilt? What if the sin is not local but systemic? Two things will then follow. First, the community, while rightly identifying some symptoms, has got the diagnosis wrong. Second, the proposed cure will not work.

There is also a third issue. The tendency to get the diagnosis wrong by focusing on a localized target may itself be a symptom of the systemic infection. The tendency to attribute blame to individuals may itself be a symptom of systemic sin. Perhaps the woman is a scapegoat.

The word 'scapegoat' entered the English language with Tyndale's translation of Leviticus in the 1530s. Tyndale invented this term as a translation of the Hebrew *Azazel*, which refers to one of a pair of goats used in the Day of Atonement ritual in Leviticus 16. The term has moved quite some way from its original rather technical usage,[21] and has been extended from simple noun to verb. 'Scapegoating' is now understood to refer to a social dynamic in which a group chooses an arbitrary individual or sub-group to blame for problems that are actually much more diffuse in origin and focus (for instance, blaming asylum-seekers for rising unemployment).

This modern understanding of the scapegoat has been developed as a perspective on the saving work of Christ by the French cultural analyst René Girard.[22] In his theory of *mimesis* Girard argues that it is not so much external pressures on a community that lead to scapegoating, but internal pressures arising from unconscious envy. (This is psychological language but it clearly is connected with the theological idea of sin.)

Girard holds that all our relationships are based around imitation of those we love and admire. This begins with parental relationships but extends to relationships with peers, teachers and so on. We want to be like 'the other'. But there is another tendency that soon emerges; an envious desire to be *better* than 'the other'. This rivalry causes conflict between pairs of individuals or among whole communities, which could potentially destroy the relationship or community. So, when conflict arises, an arbitrary external source – a scapegoat – is identified and then violently expelled. Peace is restored. But it is a temporary peace and it is based on a lie.

The whole process is unconscious. The individuals or communities involved sincerely believe that the scapegoat is the cause of the problem. Girard pointed out that this process is maintained because the scapegoat chosen is often plausible. He may be stigmatized in some way by physical appearance or ethnic origin (indeed Girard argues that communities may tolerate incomers such as Tamar because it is always useful to have a ready source of scapegoats at one's disposal); she may be too disempowered to be able to voice a defence; he may be guilty of an unrelated crime or have a history of disturbed behaviour.

Because scapegoating is superficially plausible and works in the short term, Girard asserts that it has found its way into all human cultures, and can especially be seen in the myths and rituals of human religions. But, he says, Judaism has within it the seeds of liberation from slavery to scapegoating, for there are repeated signs in the Hebrew Scriptures that God is in solidarity with those who are blamed by others. For Girard these are precursors of something that finds its fulfilment in Jesus. Jesus is a scapegoat who is put to death for the good of the wider community (John 11.50). But, crucially, Jesus is a scapegoat who is clearly and uniquely *innocent* (2 Corinthians 5.21). Jesus' innocence is proved by his resurrection. The resurrection of Jesus both vindicates him and exposes the violent process of scapegoating once and for all as a lie, and the whole system is purged of its violence. This is how God defeats human systemic sin.

Girard's analysis has not been without its critics,[23] and it is only one of a number of ways of understanding the atoning work of God in Christ. However, it does seem particularly applicable to the case of the woman taken in adultery because Jesus' response to her accusers invites them to shift the focus of exposure from her to themselves.[24] Jesus talks of sin not as located exclusively in this one woman, but as more broadly distributed among the individuals who make up the group who accompany her. He suggests that the woman is not alone in her sin. Sin infects the whole community system.

This is a simple, if radical, diagnosis. It fits with Jesus' general teaching that people need to look at themselves first before they blame others (Matthew 7.1–5; Luke 18.9–14). This not only makes for personal integrity and humility, it is the mark of a community life from which scapegoating is absent. Notice that Jesus does *not* suggest that the systemic sin cannot be localized in individuals: he invites each of the individuals who make up the group to examine his own conscience. Each individual must decide if he is in a position to cast the first stone. Jesus' first response was not to collude with the shaming of the woman. His second response is to break the group mentality down into a series of individual mindsets.

This is tremendously clever. The group is unanimous about blaming the woman. On Girard's analysis this holds the mimetic rivalry between its members in check. But the group unanimity is likely to melt away if one of its members breaks ranks and claims to be without sin. The rivalry could erupt and the individual be denounced as a hypocrite. So, from the point of view of each individual, making a claim of personal innocence would just be too risky.

Jesus does not say, 'The law of Moses is wrong.' He does not say, 'This woman is innocent.' He does not even say, 'You are no better than she.' His response is an oblique, 'First, look at yourselves.' In taking this approach Jesus saves himself from entrapment, he saves the woman from a death sentence, and he offers the whole community the means of salvation.

Jesus invites the woman's accusers to look at things from a different perspective, and in so doing he offers them a chance of insight. This is the sort of insight achieved by Judah when he finally realized that the woman he had thought was a temple prostitute was in fact his dependent kinswoman Tamar. Judah had scapegoated Tamar for the death of Onan, a death that had actually occurred because of Onan's envy of his brother Er. She was, after all, good scapegoat material, being both a foreigner and a woman. Judah came to see that, while Tamar was not entirely innocent, 'She is more in the right than I . . .' (Genesis 38.26, NRSV). He was forced to look at himself, and he did not altogether like what he saw.

The shaming spotlight is turned from the woman's body on to the inner motives of her accusers. We can infer that they feel something like shame because, one by one, they remove themselves from the public gaze. But with this shame comes the chance of freedom from self-deception, and true insight: 'If we say that we have no sin, we deceive ourselves, and the truth is not in us' (1 John 1.8, NRSV).

The sort of insight that involves an acknowledgement of personal sin is a sign of integrity. It is, paradoxically, a symptom of true wholesomeness. It is the beginning of faith, for it involves an admission that help is needed if the individual is to be sustained and healed. The community represented by 'the scribes and Pharisees' thought that it could maintain its own wholesomeness by scapegoating one woman. Jesus shows that in fact what it needs is to turn (and keep turning) and receive wholesomeness in all its parts from God.

The episode of the woman taken in adultery is, in a deep sense, an anticipation of the cross and resurrection. There is violent death in the air. There is a scapegoated victim who has many points of contact with and resemblance to Jesus. And there is Jesus himself, who unquestionably shows the scapegoating to be a lie, and so offers life to all involved.

There is scapegoating and there is solidarity. As we have seen, Jesus' family heritage, which is a good part of who he is, gives him a natural solidarity with this woman. The incarnation is, of course, an act of solidarity with all humanity. The special circumstances of Jesus' birth mean that there is a special solidarity with 'such women'. It is not until the cross itself that Jesus' solidarity with those who are stigmatized and scapegoated is fully manifested, but there are clear pointers to that solidarity here.

Jesus saves the day by exposing the scapegoating, and he raises the woman by his solidarity with her, a scapegoat like himself. (The fact that the woman may be technically or morally guilty of adultery makes her no less a scapegoat.) The suffering of a woman accused of shameful sexual crimes is seen to be in the same domain as the suffering of the cross.

Matthew seems to be aware of this as he writes his passion narrative, for he weaves into it several references to the story of Susanna, a woman falsely accused of adultery and sentenced to death.[25] Alongside this there is the steady beat of Psalm 22. In the previous chapter I noted that the psalmist was a man hemmed in by enemies who might well have been foreigners. Jesus quotes the opening words of this psalm on the cross, and here the enemies are his human accusers and executioners, and the powers of darkness. But the words of the psalm hit home again with renewed force as giving voice to the feelings of the woman, who in this episode is largely silent. They hit home as expressive of the predicament of women and men who still throughout the world are at the mercy of shaming acts of public violence:

> My God, my God, why have you forsaken me?
>> Why are you so far from helping me, from the words of my groaning?
> O my God, I cry by day, but you do not answer;
>> and by night, but find no rest.
>
> Yet you are holy,
>> enthroned on the praises of Israel.
> In you our ancestors trusted;
>> they trusted, and you delivered them.
> To you they cried, and were saved;
>> in you they trusted, and were not put to shame.

But I am a worm, and not human;
  scorned by others, and despised by the people.
All who see me mock at me;
  they make mouths at me, they shake their heads;
'Commit your cause to the LORD; let him deliver –
  let him rescue the one in whom he delights!'

Yet it was you who took me from the womb;
  you kept me safe on my mother's breast.
On you I was cast from my birth,
  and since my mother bore me you have been my God.
Do not be far from me,
  for trouble is near
  and there is no one to help.

Many bulls encircle me,
  strong bulls of Bashan surround me;
they open wide their mouths at me,
  like a ravening and roaring lion.

I am poured out like water,
  and all my bones are out of joint;
my heart is like wax;
  it is melted within my breast;
my mouth is dried up like a potsherd,
  and my tongue sticks to my jaws;
  you lay me in the dust of death.

For dogs are all around me;
  a company of evildoers encircles me.
My hands and feet have shrivelled;
I can count all my bones.
They stare and gloat over me.

(Psalm 22.1–17, NRSV)

Jesus does not stand above this woman and offer her forgiveness. He stands alongside her in her suffering. When her
accusers have departed he finally looks up in order to speak to

her rather than to speak about her. He says two things. First, she is free *from* condemnation. Second, she is free *to* live her life. The salvation that he achieved is not simply the avoidance of a death sentence, it is the gift of life. The word of release that Jesus uses – *poreuou* – is commonly found in his dismissal of those who have come to him in faith and been healed (Luke 5.24; 7.22; 8.48; 17.19; John 4.50). It means not so much 'go away' but 'go on *the way*'. It is also a word of commission (Matthew 10.6; 21.2; Luke 10.37; John 20.17). For Jesus, healing and calling to a life of discipleship – the way – are intimately linked, as we shall see in Chapter 6.

Some commentators read Jesus' injunction to the woman to 'sin no more' as inappropriately stern – especially as he has not demanded this of her accusers. It makes more sense in this context to understand it as a sign of a new relationship within which it is appropriate to make such demands. Jesus is calling the woman to a particular life of discipleship. We do not know if she accepts the call. If she does, the final verses of Psalm 22 – so like Mary's Magnificat – come into their own:

> I will tell of your name to my brothers and sisters;
>   in the midst of the congregation I will praise you:
> You who fear the Lord, praise him!
>   All you offspring of Jacob, glorify him;
>   stand in awe of him, all you offspring of Israel!
> For he did not despise or abhor
>   the affliction of the afflicted;
> he did not hide his face from me,
>   but heard when I cried to him.
>
> From you comes my praise in the great congregation;
>   my vows I will pay before those who fear him.
> The poor shall eat and be satisfied;
>   those who seek him shall praise the Lord.
>   May your hearts live for ever!

All the ends of the earth shall remember
    and turn to the Lord;
and all the families of the nations
    shall worship before him.
For dominion belongs to the Lord,
    and he rules over the nations.

To him, indeed, shall all who sleep in the earth bow down;
    before him shall bow all who go down to the dust,
    and I shall live for him.
Posterity will serve him;
    future generations will be told about the Lord,
and proclaim his deliverance to a people yet unborn,
    saying that he has done it.

(Psalm 22.22–31, NRSV)

4

Jesus sees

Deep calls to deep

As he drew near to the gate of the city, look! – a dead person being carried out for burial. He was his mother's only son, and she was a widow, and a good-sized crowd from the city was with her. Having seen her, the Lord was gutted for her and said to her, 'Don't cry!' (Luke 7.12–13)

So when Mary came where Jesus was, having seen him, she fell at his feet saying to him, 'Lord, if you had been here, my brother would not have died.' As Jesus saw her weeping, and the group of Judaeans who had come with her weeping, he let out a deep groan of anguish and was greatly troubled within himself. And he said, 'Where have you laid him?' They said to him, 'Lord, come and see.' Jesus wept. (John 11.32–35)

So, Jesus having seen his mother, and the beloved disciple standing there, says to his mother, 'Woman, look – your son.' Then he says to the disciple, 'Look – your mother.' And from that hour the disciple took her as his own. (John 19.26–27)

We saw in the previous chapter that there were special reasons for a sense of connection between Jesus and the woman taken in adultery, particular common aspects of their histories and situations that opened up the possibility of solidarity between them. This chapter explores another aspect of connection between Jesus and human beings, less bound to specific circumstances. This is Jesus' emotional response to the human condition. The story of the woman taken in adultery is marked

57

by an absence of comment on the emotional state of any of the protagonists, so these must be inferred. There are, however, several other places in the Gospels where the emotional state of Jesus is made explicit. The gospel writers never wasted words. When they include a comment on Jesus' emotions it is not as background colour but a substantial detail that merits further consideration.

The most common word used to describe the feelings of Jesus is *splanchnizomai*, usually translated 'to have compassion', something we might understand as empathy. Empathy is a characteristic of personal interactions that, like sympathy, involves making a connection with another person, seeing things from his point of view. But it goes beyond sympathy in involving emotion at least as much as 'head knowledge'. Empathy is greatly prized by psychological therapists because a high degree of accurate therapist empathy with the client has been found to predict good therapeutic outcome.[1] It requires an act of imagination that enables the therapist to stand in the client's shoes and, in some small way, *feel* what the client is feeling. It is a profound kind of affective knowing; deep calling to deep. It is one of the things that makes for solidarity.

Like all emotions, empathy is not an a priori state, it is a reaction. You can have sympathy for someone you have read or heard about. But you need to see[2] a person to have empathy with him; for empathy is a response that happens in the felt presence of another person.

The word *splanchnizomai* is difficult to pronounce and sounds ugly. It is onomatopoeic; its guttural sound matches its literal meaning which is 'of the innards and entrails'. It thus conveys emotion in all its physical fullness. It also includes a component of sympathy. The slang expression 'gutted for you' sums this up quite well. The gospel writers are therefore describing a degree of emotion that is a more extreme and dramatic version of the deep empathy of good counsellors and psychotherapists.

This feeling is attributed to Jesus on occasions when he encountered crowds of needy people (Matthew 9.36; 14.14; 15.32; Mark 6.34; 8.2), a blind man (Matthew 20.34), a leper (Mark 1.41), and the widow of Nain (Luke 7.13). On half of these occasions his feeling of compassion is said to follow directly from his *seeing* these people. The feeling is also attributed in the parables to those characters who stand for God as they encounter a human being in distress: the master of the unmerciful servant (Matthew 18.27), the good Samaritan (Luke 10.33)[3] and the father of the prodigal son (Luke 15.20). In the two Lucan parables the feeling specifically follows directly from *seeing* the person in distress. John uses a different vocabulary, but in his description of Jesus' encounter with the bereaved Mary of Bethany there is a similar very physical description of Jesus' emotion evoked on seeing her weeping. Meeting and seeing lead to deep feeling; feeling then leads immediately to action. Jesus sees, is gutted, and acts.

The people who confront Jesus have needs. The individuals and crowds who move him so deeply are sick people, hungry people and lost people – 'harassed and helpless, like sheep without a shepherd' (Matthew 9.36, NRSV). Mary of Bethany and the widow of Nain are bereaved, having lost not only a beloved relative but also their only source of male protection from danger and destitution. These people are confronted by the limits of the human condition – 'Where is the next meal coming from?'; 'What am I going to do without the bread-winner?'; 'Who will protect me from harm now?'; 'Will I ever get well?'; 'Am I going to die?'; 'Dear God, help me.' Jesus presumably understands all about the human condition, yet as he sees evidence of it everywhere he apprehends it in a new way, and it appears to cause him great distress.

We can only speculate about Jesus' precise feelings – the affective tone of 'compassion'. There seems to be a deep sadness as he weeps alongside Mary of Bethany. There seems to be a warm loving-kindness as he requests the widow of Nain to cease her tears. But there is also a suggestion of anger. The groan that he makes on seeing Mary weeping is in part a kind of snort of indignation.[4] Jesus looks on the suffering of real human beings and it makes him angry. At the most profound level he seems to be thinking, 'It shouldn't be this way!' This is the kind of reaction shown by Bob Geldof as he saw the effects of the Ethiopian famine in 1984, which crucially resulted in almost immediate dramatic action on his part. This kind of anger can be highly productive, moving quickly as it does from 'Things shouldn't be this way!' to 'Things don't have to be this way!'

But who is Jesus angry with? Perhaps he is angry with the fallen state of the world, with Satan, with the injustice of the Roman authorities, or with the hypocrisy of his own religious hierarchy. Perhaps he is angry with – or at least in conflict with – himself. He has certainly been blamed by Mary and Martha for the death of Lazarus. There seems to be a sense in which Jesus feels responsible for the situation of these people, if not as the cause then as the one who has the primary duty of care:

> I myself will be the shepherd of my sheep, and I will make them lie down, says the Lord GOD. I will seek the lost, and I will bring back the strayed, and I will bind up the injured, and I will strengthen the weak, but the fat and the strong I will destroy. I will feed them with justice.   (Ezekiel 34.15–16, NRSV)

Unlike the prophets before him, who spoke in the name of the Lord to denounce and lament over wrongdoing, and to communicate God's desire to make things right, Jesus seems to feel that *he* is the one to make things right. And as he sets about this work his full identity emerges and is made real.

This is a man whose intimate experience of the divine is of loving goodness, beauty, truth and life. He knows the Father. Yet what he sees in the world is at such deep odds with what he knows that it causes him gut-wrenching emotional anguish.

And he feels compelled to make it right. So, wherever he encounters human distress he heals, forgives, feeds. He also teaches the truth about God; for as Jesus changes situations, he shows clearly that things both shouldn't and don't have to be the way they are. He gives people an aspiration to something different, he opens up other options. The anger of Jesus is part of the pain of the incarnation, of God knocking up against the limited human frame of reference he has chosen to inhabit. It is a symptom of his vision of a real alternative, a repudiation of both fatalism and the paralysing 'if only' mindset – the one that says, 'If you had been here, my brother would not have died.' It starts in a small way with the changing of water to wine and progresses little by little until it culminates in the changing of the dead to the living.

In his Gospel John presents Jesus not only as the original creator of the cosmos (1.3) but also as the one who comes into the human situation to recreate it.[5] For John, Jesus' work of seeking and saving the lost is a recapitulation of creation, a reconstruction of human beings into the creatures that they should be. This work is painful for all involved. However, it is likened to the productive labour of childbirth (3.3; 16.21) rather than the destructive pain of illness because the suffering is transformative (12.24). It began with the birth of the cosmos (1.3), continues in the incarnation (5.17), and finishes on the cross (19.30). This Gospel has many resonances with the creation narrative of Genesis 1: there are six transformative life-giving works (changing water to wine, healing an official's son, healing a paralysed man, feeding the 5,000, healing a man born blind, raising Lazarus), there is the final glory of the cross, and then a Sabbath rest in the tomb. There is an emphasis on working during daylight hours (9.4), and of course the very first words of the Gospel, *en archē*, are identical with the first words of Genesis in the Greek Old Testament.

This perspective on the work of Jesus enhances the accounts of the other gospel writers, who describe Jesus' compassion as a response to seeing that things are wrong, and evidence of a pressing drive to make things right. John adds the insight that this making right can be understood as a series of transformative acts of *re-creation*. Once we see that the nature of Jesus' work is essentially life-giving and creative, we can begin to understand why he seems to have a particular empathy with and concern for *mothers* who mourn.

Blessed are the childless women

As we saw in Chapter 2, the pain experienced by Mary as part of her life with Jesus is clearly communicated in Luke's Gospel, and hinted at in the others. It is John who tells us that Jesus looked down from the cross and showed concern for his mother. Indeed, according to John, making sure that his mother was cared for was the rather mundane final act of Jesus' epic work of re-creation (19.28). Jesus was Mary's eldest son, and as such he had a particular duty of care for her.[6] She was presumably a widow, and therefore in much the same situation as that of the widow of Nain, deprived of her male protector. Indeed she would have been more vulnerable because of her association with a convicted and executed criminal.

The vulnerability of women deprived of male protection and material support is something that has changed little in two millennia, despite the sexual revolution of the late twentieth century in the 'developed' world. It was certainly there in the early nineteenth-century world of Jane Austen: Mrs Bennet's greatest and perfectly reasonable fear was the untimely death of her husband before alternative male providers could be found for herself and her daughters. Losing a man – son, husband or brother – was and still is a cause of both grief for loss and fear for the future. Moreover, losing a man was all too common at the time of Jesus and remains so in many parts of the world. Women in nearly all cultures live longer than men and young men are more at risk of violent death than young women.

Yet there is more to the distress of bereaved women than the loss of potential or actual breadwinners and protectors: there are feelings that spring from their experience of motherhood. Women are afforded a particular insight into the precious and precarious nature of human life because they carry it from its flickering beginnings within their wombs for nine months, and experience the overwhelming and relentless power of its departure from their bodies as it enters the world as a fully formed, if completely dependent, human being whom they tenderly shelter against their breasts. For many years they watch over their fragile charges, nurturing, providing a secure base from which they can go out into the world little by little, and to which they can return again and again when a safe haven is required. Their work is a work of careful creation. This is costly, for a foetus and breastfeeding infant is literally built out of its mother's body, and the process of pregnancy, labour and parenting is hazardous and physically demanding. There are psychological demands too, for there must be an ever-present alertness to the dangers that may lie in wait for the naive and vulnerable child if he is to survive into adolescence and adulthood. And if, despite all of her efforts, the hazards of life intervene, and the child, adolescent, or young adult is snuffed out, the mother's terrible grief is not just about the loss of the dearly beloved, not just about the loss of a potential source of care and protection, it is also a great anger at the waste of all that creative and costly work:[7]

'O how wretched am I and many times unhappy! After bearing seven children, I am now the mother of none! O seven childbirths all in vain, seven profitless pregnancies, fruitless nurturings and wretched nursings! In vain, my sons, I endured many birth pangs for you, and the more grievous anxieties of your upbringing. Alas for my children, some unmarried, others married and without offspring. I shall not see your children or have the happiness of being called grandmother. Alas, I who had so many and beautiful children am a widow and alone,

with many sorrows. And when I die, I shall have none of my
sons to bury me.' (4 Maccabees 16.6–11, NRSV)

The mourning of children is one of the works of women that
is attested to in the Hebrew Scriptures (Genesis 21.16; 1 Kings
17.18; Jeremiah 31.15).[8] In the New Testament Matthew picks
up the theme of Rachel's lament in his account of the slaughter
of the innocents (Matthew 2.16–18).[9] As we have seen, the
Gospels tell of Mary of Nazareth and the widow of Nain, and
they also describe the grief of Martha and Mary of Bethany in
some detail. These sisters had not technically lost a child, but it
is likely that Lazarus was a much younger brother, as Martha
was the head of the household (Luke 10.38). This seems to have
been a family in which two older female siblings cared for a
younger male sibling. Finally, Luke's Gospel describes another
group of mourning women: the 'daughters of Jerusalem' (Luke
23.27–28). These women are among a crowd, lamenting the
approaching death of Jesus. But Jesus addresses them and turns
their attention from him to their children, to the motherly task
of mourning. His words to them culminate in a radical beatitude, often translated, 'Blessed are the barren.' This builds on
five previous beatitudes in Luke's Gospel. The first four have
been addressed to Jesus' disciples, and reassure them that those
who suffer poverty, hunger, grief and persecution on account of
him are all blessed (Luke 6.20–22). The fifth is addressed to a
woman in the crowd who expresses her admiration of Jesus by
blessing his biological mother (Luke 11.28). This beatitude and
'blessed are the barren' are placed together in the *Gospel of
Thomas*,[10] and in this way it is easier to see their sense:

> A woman from the crowd said to him, 'Blessed is the womb that
> gave birth to you and the breasts which fed you.' He said,
> 'Blessed are those who hear the word of the Father and keep
> it in truth. For there will be days when you will say, "Blessed
> is the womb that did not give birth and the breasts that did
> not feed."' (*Gospel of Thomas* 79)

The beatitudes of Jesus make powerful use of paradox to communicate a radical inversion of values. They are markers of the breaking in of the kingdom that he proclaims. Jesus is bringing in a new age, and his coming marks the transition from the old to the new, a kind of pivot point, a liminal moment of rapid change when things are turned upon their head.[11]

This is rather like the tossing of a pancake; what was on top will be underneath and what was underneath will be on top. The king of all is servant of all; the first will be last and the last first; the poor will be rich and the rich poor; the hungry will be full and the full hungry; those who mourn will laugh and those who laugh will mourn; those who are hated will be revered and those who are revered will be forgotten; those at the periphery will be at the centre and those at the centre will fall off the edge (Matthew 5.2–12; 18.1–2; 19.30 and parallels; Luke 6.24–26; 13.28–29; 16.22–23; 22.26–27). These cataclysmic changes are the birth pangs of a new age and it is all deeply disorienting:[12]

> Peter began to say to him, 'Look, we have left everything and followed you.'
>
> Jesus said, 'Truly I say to you, there is no one who has left house or brothers or sisters or mother or father or children or land, for the sake of me and for the sake of the good news, but will receive a hundredfold now in this age – houses, brothers and sisters, mothers and children, and land with persecutions – and in the age to come eternal life. So, many who are first will be last, and the last first.' Now they were on the road going up to Jerusalem, and Jesus was going ahead of them, and they were amazed, but those following were afraid.   Mark 10.28–32a

Life in these transitional times, the end of the old order, is not subject to the conventional terms of reference that held good in more stable periods.[13] The building of family life through marriage and procreation, the dwelling-spirituality of settlement in one place, has given way to a spirituality of journeying, with fellow travellers constituting the new family unit (Matthew 8.19–22; Luke 9.57–60). As part of this new order, the lone woman unencumbered by the practical and emotional ties of children achieves a new status.[14] Conditions that were once shameful – 'spinster', 'barren' – or low status and dependent – 'widow' – are now highly valued.

There is a kind of casual pragmatism about this. Precisely because Jesus sees that mothers are hostages to fate, indeed feels the inconsolable pain of bereaved mothers, he recognizes the benefits of childlessness. A woman without exclusive human emotional ties can focus on her discipleship in a way not open to a woman with a husband and children. Paul too expresses this idea (1 Corinthians 7.34).

Pragmatism is also evident in the story of the great banquet (Matthew 22.2–14; Luke 14.16–24). The 'undesirables' are invited to dinner simply because the usual suspects have declined the invitation and the banquet needs to go ahead. Just as there is no positive discrimination in favour of 'the poor, the crippled, the blind, and the lame', there is no positive discrimination in favour of lone women. They just turn out to be well fitted for a central place in the kingdom, and because God in Jesus is operating a level playing field, they find their place.

This is simply the way things are, the outcome of circumstances. Yet it offers new options for lone women both in terms of what they can do and the way they see themselves. It is out of pragmatic responses to new circumstances that new insights and perspectives often arise, bringing with them genuine liberation for some. The most obvious example is the achievement of the vote for women in Britain beginning in 1918, which was at least partly a result of the social upheaval of the Great War. This was something that had not been accomplished by many years of active political campaign in the period before the war.[15]

Despite the inverted values of the kingdom preached by Jesus, the churches today are not so different from wider society in their attitude to lone women. There is in our culture a widespread suspicion of single women. There is also a disgusted horror of menopausal women and a deeply patronizing attitude to old women.[16] Where they are not under the control of a male (be this husband, father or bishop), single childless women are a common cause for concern. They may be seen as potential predators of married men, and are always at some level despised for their lack of procreative power. Women whose childbearing days are over are frequently stereotyped as dried up and 'past their sell-by date', sitting sadly in empty nests, their contribution to society limited to the adjunctive care of grandchildren. The 'frustrated old bag' figure exemplified by Mrs Doyle,[17] the widow who keeps house for Father Ted and his colleagues, seems to be a version of a powerful Jungian witch archetype[18] that has been deprived of its mystery or danger, and is thus merely pitiful. The character of Mary in *Pride and Prejudice* seems destined to grow up into this role, a rather fussy spinster condemned to spend many years caring for her demanding mother.

It is therefore interesting, and something of an indictment of present-day attitudes, that Luke's Gospel tells us that the first older lone woman encountered by the infant Jesus is not his babysitting granny or housekeeper, but the prophet Anna. Anna was a widow of many years' standing, freed by the menopause to inhabit the Temple continuously in order to pursue an exemplary life of piety.[19] Following her encounter with Jesus her status is raised still further as she preaches about his coming to all who are seeking the liberation of Jerusalem (Luke 2.38). She is the first Christian prophet.

Anna is the first of many lone women, young and old, who were involved in the early Church, women who had more freedom than their married and childbearing counterparts to follow Jesus on the way.[20] She provides a positive model for older women, showing that there are viable alternatives for them outside of the family circle. She embarked upon a post-domestic life in the sacred space of the Temple and, like the sparrow in Psalm 84, she found a nest for herself in the courts of the Lord. She exemplifies a phenomenon that has frequently been observed by those who study development across the lifespan; the emergence of a concern with existential and spiritual issues in mid to late life.[21] The psychological resources that are needed to support this are at their peak during this life phase. They include finely tuned powers of discernment and an awareness of a range of perspectives and practical approaches that can be applied to life's problems – in other words, *wisdom*.[22]

But however wise and pious Anna was, she was still restricted to the court of the women, and it may be that she missed her husband and mourned lost children, or children she never had. The freedom of lone women is a freedom from the worries that go with attachment and responsibility, but it is not a freedom from all pain. Women who – for whatever reason – are not in an exclusive, intimate and permanent relationship with a partner, women who have not been able to conceive or carry a baby to term, women who have lost or lost touch with their children, can experience intense grief for what might have been, profound loneliness and feelings of rejection and worthlessness.

Such feelings are by no means trivial, and they are raised up by Jesus as he laments over Jerusalem. When Jesus sees Jerusalem he weeps (Luke 19.41), just as he did when confronted by Mary of Bethany. The words of lament that sum up the reason for his tears are these: 'Jerusalem, Jerusalem, killing the prophets and stoning those sent to you! How often have I wanted to gather your children as a hen her brood under her wings, and you did not want it!' (Luke 13.34; and see Matthew 23.37).

In other words – 'I so wanted to be your mum but you wouldn't let me.' The grief of Jesus is this time not empathy with women mourning what they have lost, not even empathy with women yearning for what they have been denied;

it is the grief *of* a woman yearning for what she has been denied. This is the voice of *Sophia*, the wisdom of God, who is always spoken of in feminine terms. She has children (Luke 7.35), sometimes likened to a brood of chickens.[23] However, as she makes overtures to Jerusalem, she is rejected (Luke 11.49). *Sophia* is best thought of as one of the ways that God acts in the cosmos. When God acts creatively and benevolently *Sophia* is at work. *Sophia*'s children are God's creative and providential works (Proverbs 3.19–20). So, if Jesus identifies himself with *Sophia*, he is identifying himself with God's right-hand woman (Proverbs 8.30; Ecclesiasticus 24), perhaps even with God herself. As Jesus-the-mother-hen laments the long and fruitless history of God's sending emissaries to Jerusalem, he is talking from an eternal divine perspective. His words here are almost as highly charged as, 'Before Abraham was, I AM' (John 8.58). And in addition, their tone is feminine.

The character of the Lord as experienced throughout the history of the people of Israel has attributes of both the 'masculine' and the 'feminine'. However, the biological constraint of being one sex (and therefore not the other) is one of the many limitations endured by God in Jesus through the incarnation. There is no question about Jesus' sex; he was male.

But Jesus' gendered identity turns out to be more complex. For the more closely he is identified with the Lord, the more space there is for a mix of 'masculine' and 'feminine' traits to emerge and develop.

Sex is a biological given. But gendered identity is, like other aspects of personal identity, something that is constructed by the individual in negotiation with those around him in the context of cultural expectations. Jesus and the first Christian communities had both 'masculine' and 'feminine' concepts with which to inform their understanding of his identity,[24] and they appear to have made use of both[25] (for instance, the masculine *huios tou theou* (Son of God) and the feminine *sophia tou theou* (Wisdom of God)). They could presumably do this because Jesus the human being was amenable to both perspectives.

Definitions of 'masculinity' and 'femininity' vary across cultures and generations, and so it would be anachronistic to describe Jesus as a 'feminine' man. It perhaps makes more sense to observe that the Gospels present us with a male Jesus who has a propensity to see things from the point of view of females:

- Jesus has a particular empathy with female varieties of distress – the anxiety of mothers and the grief and frustration of lone women.
- Jesus values children.
- Jesus forms intimate relationships with people of both sexes.
- Jesus talks about himself in maternal terms, covering and protecting his offspring, nurturing his followers from his own body, and literally feeling broody.
- Jesus' work is understood as an act of creation.
- Jesus is understood to be God's agent, his beloved only son *and* his right-hand woman.[26]

Seeing things differently

The values of the kingdom of God are inverted, and entering the kingdom means seeing things differently (Mark 4.11–12). In almost every respect Jesus seems to have seen things differently from those around him, needed to help his followers to see things his way, and continually expressed his astonishment that it was so difficult for them (for instance, Matthew 16.9 and parallels).

Jesus was a keen observer of the physical and social world. His teaching is the result of extended observation of the ways of the weather, of the animals and plants of his homeland, and of the ways human beings treat each other. Jesus was a country lad, and in Mark's Gospel we are told that when he arrives in the great city of Jerusalem the first thing he does is to look around (Mark 11.11). Jesus carefully watches the way people behave in the Temple precincts, and it clearly disturbs him. But he isn't overwhelmed by the ostentatious and obvious; he notices something hidden and small. He notices a poor lone woman placing two coins in the treasury (Mark 12.41–43; Luke 21.1–4). He draws her actions to the attention of his disciples and says essentially, 'Look! What is small is big, what is big is small.' In rural Galilee he has reflected on this fact using the mustard seed to help him communicate his insight into the upside-down nature of the kingdom. In urban Jerusalem he sees and communicates the same thing, this time drawing on a little woman rather than on a little seed to make his point.

Jesus' vision seems to have been attuned to the small and the peripheral, and to the discernment of hidden potential. These characteristics come together in the tax collector Zacchaeus, who was both small of stature and socially marginalized, yet who actually had much to offer.[27] As Jesus passes along the road through Jericho he looks up and notices Zacchaeus (Luke 19.5). Nobody else has taken notice of him, but Jesus sees him, sees his potential to change, and calls to him. Something very similar happens with Matthew, who is sitting in the tax collector's booth (Matthew 9.9) and who like Zacchaeus is seen and then called. Both these unpromising individuals end up bearing good fruit.

In the next chapter we consider another unpromising individual whose potential is spotted by Jesus, and who ends up bearing good fruit: the Samaritan woman he encounters at Jacob's well. But perhaps the most unpromising of all is Jairus' daughter. Everyone thinks she is dead. She is not worth troubling an important man with (Mark 5.35; Luke 8.49). In the eyes of the bystanders she was, after all, only a daughter, and thus more disposable in the greater scheme of things than a son and heir. Perhaps as a result of wishful thinking, the professional mourners have already begun their work. Here the dissonance between Jesus' view that the child is asleep and ready to be awakened, and the view of the mourners that she is dead and worthless, is so great that they laugh at him (Matthew 9.24 and parallels). But they do not see what Jesus sees: a little girl who must be called and raised up simply because she's worth it.

5

Jesus knows

———◆•◆•———

To know is to love

It's to do with knowing and being known. I remember how it
stopped seeming odd that in biblical Greek knowing was used
for making love. Who-sit knew so and so. Carnal knowledge.
It's what lovers trust each other with. Knowledge of each other,
not in the flesh but through the flesh, knowledge of self, the
real him, the real her, *in extremis* the mask slipped from the
face. Every other version of oneself is on offer to the public.
We share our vivacity, grief, sulks, anger, joy . . . we hand it out
to anybody who happens to be standing around, to friends and
family with a momentary sense of indecency perhaps, to
strangers with hesitation. Our lovers share us with the passing
trade. But in pairs we insist that we give ourselves to each other.
What selves? What's left? What else is there that hasn't been
dealt out like a deck of cards? A sort of knowledge. Personal,
final, uncompromised. Knowing, being known. I revere that.[1]

The character of Henry from Tom Stoppard's *The Real Thing*
is correct when he says that the Greek word *ginōskō* is used in
the Bible to refer to sexual relations. It is used in this way
in the New Testament, for instance in Matthew 1.25 and Luke
1.34. This follows on naturally from its use in the Septuagint,
the Greek version of the Jewish Scriptures. The Septuagint
itself has *ginōskō* as a translation of the Hebrew word *yādaᶜ*
(see for instance Genesis 4.1). Dictionaries give a range of
meanings for the word *ginōskō*: 'have knowledge of ', 'find out',
'learn', 'understand', 'perceive', 'discern', 'recognize', 'remember'.

The Hebrew *yāda^c* has a similar range of meanings, but also some additional overtones. It can be used in the context of an interpersonal relationship meaning to choose or select (e.g. Genesis 18.19) and to care about or be concerned for (2 Samuel 7.20).

For the biblical writers, to 'know' another person means to have a particular sort of intimacy with her – one that involves choosing her over and against alternatives in order to be in a special relationship. Monogamous marriage is perhaps the best present-day illustration of this kind of relationship. For the writers of the Hebrew Scriptures, however, the prototypical relationship of knowing is that between God and his people. Both human marriage and the relationship between God and his people are understood to be exclusive intimate love relationships that are essentially impenetrable to others.

Psalm 139 is an extended reflection on this theme – the exclusive relationship that God has with his people, expressed through a relationship with a representative individual, perhaps the warrior king David. The present-day reader is more likely to receive this psalm as the psychological response of a private individual to a sense of being known intimately by the God who made her.

> O LORD, you have searched me and known me.
> You know when I sit down and when I rise up;
> you discern my thoughts from far away.
> You search out my path and my lying down,
> and are acquainted with all my ways.
> Even before a word is on my tongue,
> O LORD, you know it completely.
> You hem me in, behind and before,
> and lay your hand upon me.
> Such knowledge is too wonderful[2] for me;
> it is so high that I cannot attain it.
>
> Where can I go from your spirit?
> Or where can I flee from your presence?

If I ascend to heaven, you are there;
    if I make my bed in Sheol, you are there.
If I take the wings of the morning
    and settle at the farthest limits of the sea,
even there your hand shall lead me,
    and your right hand shall hold me fast.
If I say, 'Surely the darkness shall cover me,
    and the light around me become night',
even the darkness is not dark to you;
    the night is as bright as the day,
    for darkness is as light to you.

For it was you who formed my inward parts;
    you knit me together in my mother's womb.
I praise you, for I am fearfully and wonderfully made.
    Wonderful are your works;
that I know very well.

(Psalm 139.1–14, NRSV)

God's knowledge of the psalmist is fundamentally the creator's knowledge of his creature. This is the creator who from the beginning has had the individual 'in mind' and who keeps remembering him (Psalm 8.4). Indeed without the creator's constant remembering the individual would cease to be. The knowledge-relationship with God is thus not an optional extra for the psalmist; it is a necessary condition of life.

But does this sense of being known by God bring comfort or discomfort? Does it bring a warm sense of love or a cold sense of dread? Is this a psalm of delight or of despair? Much depends on the psychological predispositions of the hearer.

In my practice as a clinical psychologist I have encountered many people who have a fear of intimacy with others. Often the bottom line for these people is something like this: 'If others knew what I was *really* like they would turn away in disgust.' People who hold this sort of belief spend much of their time in relationships making sure that others do not find out what they are 'really like', by keeping them at an emotional or physical distance, or by employing strategies of psychological subterfuge. When others pay them genuine compliments or seek out their company they believe that this must be because the subterfuge has worked, and their public *persona*[3] has not been rumbled: 'I've fooled them into believing that I am a lovable human being – if only they knew . . .'

This tendency to establish psychological 'private parts' that must be kept covered at all times is not confined to those who seek professional help for relationship difficulties. Rowan Williams has argued that it is ubiquitous:

> It's sometimes been said that if someone came up to you in the street and whispered, 'They've found out! Run!', nine out of ten of us would. We nearly all have secrets that we don't want exposed – even if they are quite trivial in the cold light of day – and that phrase tells us a lot, the *cold* light: we don't want to be under the kind of detached scrutiny that threatens and diminishes us, sitting under a bare light bulb and being interrogated. So when it looks as though our secrets are about to be revealed, we easily panic and run.[4]

This is the mindset that leads to terror at the thought of being known by God.[5]

Yet there is another side to being known. It can be found in the feeling of affirmation that we have when someone sends us a card or a web-link with the words, 'I saw this and thought of you,' or when someone buys us a Christmas present that really is exactly what we wanted. 'How did you guess?' we ask – 'I know you so well,' comes the reply. This other side can also be found in the company of those who know us sufficiently well to call us by a special nickname (as lovers so often do), or who use a catchphrase that has some special significance, perhaps linked to an intimate memory. It can be found in our relationships with people who help us to realize what is best in our characters by first discerning potential, and then supporting and praising signs of its development. All these things can, if we let them, bring confidence and joy, and so help us to flourish.

Many would argue that this sort of knowing is the mark of good parenting and strong friendships. It is perhaps not surprising that it is also an aspiration of many psychological therapies, particularly – though by no means exclusively – person-centred humanistic psychotherapies.[6] These approaches view the psychotherapeutic relationship as something like a functional re-parenting of the client, who is provided with optimal conditions for personal growth by the therapist. It allows the client to entertain the notion that 'The *real* me is lovable.'

This kind of knowledge evokes a delighted wonder rather than a fearful attempt to shut it out. It's the kind of wonder expressed by Nathanael when Jesus makes exactly the sort of positive discerning comment about him that we have just considered:

> Jesus saw Nathanael coming towards him, and said concerning him, 'Look! – a true Israelite in whom there is no treachery.'
> Nathanael said to him, 'How do you know me?' In reply Jesus said to him, 'Before Philip called you under the fig tree, I saw you.' Nathanael replied, 'Rabbi, you are the Son of God! – the King of Israel!' (John 1.47–49)

The Gospels present us with a picture of the kingdom of God in which people participate through being known by Jesus. This is a direct parallel with the kingdom of Israel in which the Jews participate because, as a people, they are known by the Lord. When Jesus tells Nathanael that, even before he was called by Philip, he already 'knew' him, he is indicating that Nathanael has been seen, assessed and chosen for membership of the kingdom. This may at first seem arbitrary; it seems that it's not what you know but whom you know (or who knows you) that determines whether you are in or out. However, the gospel accounts make it clear that being 'known' by Jesus is closely related to the moral quality of the individual involved. In Matthew's Gospel Jesus tells believers to 'Depart from me – I never knew you' because of their lack of love for others who are in need (Matthew 7.23). And in the case of Nathanael the 'knowing' is expressed as a judgement about Nathanael's integrity of character. Which comes first, what causes what, is not made clear. Questions of causation are probably not the right kind of questions to ask. The important point is that to be *known by* Jesus is closely tied up with *being like* Jesus in one's character and behaviour.

Later in John's Gospel Jesus describes himself as the Shepherd, and talks at length about his relationship with his flock. This is a relationship of mutual knowledge and recognition, which enables trust:

> 'He who comes through the door is the shepherd of the sheep. The doorkeeper opens for this one, and the sheep hear his voice, and he calls his own sheep by name and leads them out. When he has led out all his own he goes in front of them and the sheep follow him, for they recognize his voice. But they will not follow a stranger; on the contrary they will run away from him because they do not recognize the voice of strangers . . . My sheep hear my voice and I know them and they follow me.'
>
> (John 10.2–5, 27)

This pastoral imagery, based on a close observation of the natural world, is hugely reassuring for those who are inside the fold. It also presents the notion of 'election' in a way that undercuts the worries that some might have about predestination. For it is not a metaphor that should be used to establish a systematic theology in which certain people are elected to be saved and others are elected to be damned, with Jesus administering the process like some mindless bureaucrat. It is instead a psychological description of what it *feels like* to encounter Jesus; the feeling is a deeply affirming one of being known, of having been known for a long time, of being in an intimate and (oddly given the large numbers of people involved!) an exclusive love relationship.[7] And the feeling is one of inevitability, of encountering a soulmate. As with Elizabeth and Darcy, it just seems to be a matter of time before the relationship happens, often despite other intentions that we may have.[8] Someone once described it to me this way: 'You are completely free to choose but you have no choice at all.' The sheep are not physically tied to the shepherd, it's just that they can't help but respond to his voice.

There is a kind of freedom involved, for the sheep are being led out of the confines of the fold to the broad expanses of the hills to find pasture. But they are not being released to run randomly in any direction. The freedom is primarily a freedom to be the person God has always had 'in mind'. It's a freedom from obstacles and encumbrances that have got in the way of authentic personal flourishing, rather than a freedom from all restrictions so that we can be anything we want.

All of this, so reassuring to those who are 'in', would be equally disquieting for those who seem to be outside the flock – who by accident of birth do not fall under the care of the shepherd – were it not for the fact that the metaphor is then stretched to its limits by Jesus who says, 'But I have other sheep not of this fold' (John 10.16), presenting a picture of one shepherd who calls sheep from far and near to be part of one enormous flock. And these sheep too are known by the shepherd and respond to his voice. The definitive example presented to us in the Gospels is the Samaritan woman who encounters Jesus as she comes to draw water at Jacob's well (John 4.4–42).

As the deer longs for the water-brooks

The ancient people of Samaria, who had a reasonable claim to be the true Israelites,[9] pop up from time to time in the Gospels of John and Luke. Unlike the single brief mention that they get in Matthew's Gospel, their treatment is sympathetic. Luke and John also share other unique material, such as the characters of Mary and Martha, and it seems likely that they had access to at least one common source that was additional to those used by Mark and Matthew. It is possible that one of these sources was a group of Samaritan Christians, and some scholars have argued that John's community, for whom he wrote his Gospel, had a sizeable Samaritan membership.[10]

Many scholars find John's assertion (4.4) that Jesus journeyed through Samaria implausible. Although this was the most direct route between Judaea and Galilee,[11] it was through hilly and potentially inhospitable country. Jews tended to avoid Samaritans where possible, and if Jesus saw his mission as primarily to Jews (as implied by Matthew), an evangelistic foray in that direction seems unlikely. On this view early Christian missionaries such as Philip (Acts 8.5) brought the gospel to the Samaritans, and then a 'Jesus in Samaria' tradition was constructed retrospectively, fuelled partly by wishful thinking, in much the same way as the medieval 'Jesus in Glastonbury' tradition:[12] 'And did those feet in recent times walk upon Samaria's mountains green?'

Just as it has been argued that the setting of John's story has no roots in geographical reality, it has also been argued that the woman herself is a symbolic individual who has little or no roots in historical reality. According to this theory, the use of a female protagonist makes sense because she is representative of a people who were once in a faithful relationship to the Lord but then attached themselves to several other 'husbands' (2 Kings 17.24ff.). The woman who has had five husbands is merely a peg on whom issues of concern to Samaritan Christians might easily be hung.

There is, however, a problem with this view that the story of Jesus and the Samaritan woman is simply a literary construction whose primary aim was to address issues in an early Christian community that included Samaritans. This is the fact that John's Gospel is the only one that claims to be written by an eyewitness. Of all the Gospels it is the most geographically and socially accurate, and it is presented as history rather than story. Of course, ancient concepts of history and ancient understandings of what it means to be an eyewitness are rather different from our own.[13] John's descriptions of incidents from the life of Jesus are not video replays of historical events. They are more like extensive reflections on historical events in which the witnesses participated, reconstructions that are part of a process of sense-making. Indeed he alludes to this process (John 2.22; 12.16). But he is also clear that the process is itself grounded in witnessed events, not in his visionary imagination (e.g. John 19.35; 21.24). This writer is not so much guarding a received tradition about Jesus as communicating a memory of Jesus. If he says that Jesus passed through Samaria, initiated a conversation with a local woman at a well, and stayed in the area for two days, then this statement should be taken seriously at face value as a piece of historical evidence that stands in tension with that provided by Matthew 10.5. It cannot be simply discounted. Furthermore, John gives an explanation as to why Jesus might have taken this route homewards from Jerusalem; he had caused a rumpus in the Temple, and some controversy was developing around his relationship with John the Baptist, so he may have wanted to avoid the more public road along the Jordan valley.

Therefore in what follows, while recognizing that the Samaritan woman is surely a representative figure who stands for a particular community, I will treat her primarily as a historical individual who encountered Jesus during his ministry. Her conversation with Jesus can be helpfully understood from both these perspectives; they are not mutually exclusive. (This is not so different from the case of the Gentile woman, Canaanite in a symbolic sense, Syro-Phoenician in a historical sense.)

The encounter between Jesus and the Samaritan woman is, on the face of it, similar to many other such encounters described by John. For instance, it is the questions of individuals encountered by Jesus that often provide the occasion for his extended monologues (such as Nicodemus in 3.4, Thomas in 14.5 and Philip in 14.8). Some individuals also enter into dialogues with Jesus usually in the context of healings (like the paralytic in John 5 and the man born blind in John 9). But these dialogues are short. The encounter with the Samaritan woman is unique in being an extended dialogue, the longest by far in this Gospel, with seven utterances by Jesus and six by the woman.

One of several things that are evident in this dialogue is that the woman is coming to faith in Jesus. In many respects the story parallels the journey to faith of the man born blind in John 9, with a revelation of the true identity of Jesus made in incremental steps[14] from 'a Judaean' (4.9), through 'greater than our ancestor Jacob' (4.12), 'a prophet' (4.19), 'the Messiah' (4.25), culminating with Jesus' statement 'I AM' (4.26). But here, instead of a physical disability there is a psychological need. The woman is not blind, she is thirsty for understanding. She needs to understand and she needs to be understood. This is not evident at first, for the dialogue begins with the weary Jesus asking the woman for a drink. He seems to be the thirsty one.

There is no getting away from the erotic overtones of this scene. First, we are told that the well was in land originally purchased by Jacob (Genesis 33.19); it was by a well that Jacob first encountered and kissed the woman who was to be the love of his life (Genesis 29.10–11), and indeed the well is an obvious sexual symbol in itself (Song of Songs 4.15).[15] Second, Jesus expresses some interest in and intimate knowledge of the woman's marital and sexual history. Third, and most important, there is a kind of 'eros of the mind'[16] at work, for the dialogue is, like the well, profound. It plumbs theological depths. It is this that seems to be disturbing the male disciples when they discover Jesus 'in discourse[17] with a woman' (4.27). What's more, Jesus is not simply doing the woman the honour of instructing her like a disciple; the conversation comes over as a debate between peers, with the woman challenging Jesus at various points with 'Yes, but . . .' statements (4.11–12, 20, 25). It is intercourse as much as discourse.

The dialogue begins with Jesus' rather improper overture to the woman, who replies in some indignation (and we are not told whether she accedes to Jesus' request for a drink). She is on her home territory and he is at some disadvantage because he is a stranger. On the other hand she is vulnerable. It seems that she is alone. (It was not usual to visit the well in the noon-day heat.) She is in a place where women are known to gather regularly and need to be on guard against molestation by males. Her defensiveness is understandable.

Jesus' next statement assures her of his good intentions: 'If you had perceived the gift of God and who it is saying to you, "Give me a drink" you would have asked him and he would have given you living water.' The woman has been essentially blinded by her suspicion of Judaean males, so that the gift that this encounter offers her is veiled from her sight. She justifies her prejudice by asserting her ethnic identity as an heir of Jacob. Jesus responds, as we have already seen at the wedding at Cana, by taking an ancient sacred symbol of the Israelite heritage and transforming it into something better, different-yet-connected to what it was before. Jacob's well gives good water, but the living water provided by Jesus is better. What's more, a well is fixed in one place and people have to go to it to find water. Jesus is a dynamic source of water, who has drawn near[18] to people so that they can drink of him.

As Jesus speaks of what he can offer the woman her thirst becomes apparent; there is a shift in her attitude and an opening up of her defences. She gives him the title of *kurie*, an indication of respect. She starts to see that he may have something that she both wants and needs. But they are still talking obliquely about water. Jesus then gets to the crux of the matter by asking the woman to go and fetch her husband.

Unlike the woman taken in adultery, there is no indication that this woman has committed any acts of sexual misconduct. She has had five husbands, but that is not unheard of. She may have been a widow or an innocent divorcee. Her current partner may simply have refused to marry her. She does, however, have a history with men, and it is reasonable to infer that it is not a satisfactory history. She has been abandoned through death or desertion five times and it looks likely, given the ambiguous state of her present relationship, that this will be a continued pattern. She has not yet found a reliable man. Relationships for her, like the water in her jar, run out and leave her thirsty.

And now an unexpectedly decent man enables her to voice her problem, to say, 'I am thirsty – I have no husband.' Jesus does not diagnose the problem for her. Instead, based on his understanding of her, he sets the conditions for her *self-understanding* by asking just the right question.[19] As soon as she reaches this insight he affirms her by telling her that she is correct and that she speaks the truth. Jesus knows what this woman is 'really' like, and he expresses no disgust. On the contrary, he didn't approach her, ask for a drink, and offer her salvation because he was acting under some misapprehension about her.[20] He knew all about her issues. He knew his sheep and he called her by name. Jesus also knows what this woman might become if she is freed to be herself, as we shall shortly see.

The woman remains perplexed. She has come to see that Jesus has deep insight into her soul, but she is still inhibited from full profession of faith in him because he is a Judaean. So she gets straight to the theological point that divides Samaritans and Judaeans; the appropriate place to worship the Lord. After asserting the fact that the one who brings salvation is a

Judaean not a Samaritan, Jesus cuts right across her question. Arguments about the appropriate location to worship God have been displaced by the new age that has been inaugurated with his coming. *Now* the important question concerns the appropriate *attitude* of the worshipper. This is an attitude of personal integrity, which begins with seeing and speaking the truth, something he has just commended the woman for doing.

It is at this point that she introduces the idea of 'the Messiah'. In this she shows more dawning insight, both about the signs of the time and the identity of Jesus. She is wondering if the coming of the messiah might be near, and about to enter her awareness is the thought that she might actually be in his presence. And then Jesus delivers a bombshell, which concludes the dialogue. He makes the first of 23 'I AM' (*egō eimi*) statements that occur in John's Gospel. About half of these are followed by a predicate (for instance, 'I am the true vine', 15.1). The other half stand alone and tend to be translated 'I am he' (or 'It's me') in English Bibles. This unfortunately masks the significance that the Greek phrase *egō eimi* would have had for the first Jewish readers and hearers of the gospel. It is the phrase used in the Septuagint to translate the Hebrew *anî hû*, found several times in the book of Isaiah[21] at points where the sovereign Lord reveals his true nature as both creator and redeemer.[22] The significance of this phrase seems clear to those who come to arrest Jesus in John 18.6; they fall to the ground on hearing it.

John is telling us that Jesus makes the first self-revelation of his full divine nature to a Samaritan woman he has essentially picked up at a well. And we see that her reaction is to leave her water jar (which she metaphorically no longer needs because her thirst has been quenched), to tell the story of Jesus' knowledge of her and to invite others to consider the question of his identity. This is an apostolic action, yet conducted in a rather feminine way: not in closed propositional proclaiming, but in open wondering questioning. And we are told (4.39) that many came to faith because of her witness. She has not only had her own thirst quenched, but she has in herself the resources to quench the thirst of others. This has come about because Jesus knew her, and it is his transforming knowledge of her that convinces others to believe in him.

The woman has been raised up by her encounter with Jesus. Her eyes have been opened to his identity, her need for understanding has been met, and consequently her thirst for authentic and reliable love has been quenched. The conversation between them covers a great deal of theological ground in a short space of time, and they talk of deep spiritual realities, sometimes using the mundane language of everyday life as metaphor. There is mutual understanding and connection; they are on the same wavelength.

And we see that the male disciples, returning from their shopping trip, are still working out how to turn the radio on. They are way behind the woman. For, having got over the shock of Jesus' intercourse with her, they cannot summon up the courage to question him (unlike her), and the best title they can come up with to address him is 'Rabbi' (while she is already using the title 'Messiah'). Not only that, when Jesus presents the idea of food to them as a spiritual metaphor, the male disciples take him literally (just as the woman took the idea of water literally at the beginning of her faith journey). This Samaritan woman has been raised up ahead of and above her male Judaean counterparts.

To be recognized by Christ, to be called by name or, as in the case of this woman, by autobiographical details, is essentially to be loved. Over the centuries this has been the experience of many. An experience of this sort is what first drew me to Christ. It seems to have been a core part of the spiritual experience of Paul, who refers to it almost in passing, as if it were obvious and taken for granted. In so doing he inadvertently communicates its fundamental reality:

But now, having known God, or rather having been known by God, how can you return back again to weak and inferior rudiments? How can you want to be enslaved to them once more? (Galatians 4.9)

For now we see in a mirror obscurely, but then face to face. Now I know in part; then I shall know completely, just as I have been known completely. (1 Corinthians 13.12)

6

Jesus calls

———◆•◆———

Women's trouble

And next he was travelling through each town and village proclaiming and bringing the good news of the kingdom of God,
and also the twelve with him, and certain women who were
healed of evil spirits and weaknesses, Mary, called Magdalene,
from whom seven demons had gone out, and Joanna, the wife
of Chuza, Herod's steward, and Susanna . . .   (Luke 8.1–3a)

As we have seen, the Samaritan woman at the well was called by
Jesus and found herself proclaiming his coming among her
own people. She was a witness who invited people to come and
see the Messiah, just as Andrew had done before her (John 1.41).
The woman's mundane and routine pattern of life was interrupted by her encounter with Jesus. She left her water jar,
something that Jesus had offered to fill in a new way, and she
moved in a new direction. There is here a parallel with the
fishermen disciples whose mundane and routine pattern of
life was interrupted by the call of Jesus and who left their nets
(Matthew 4.20; Mark 1.18) – nets that Jesus was able to fill in
a new way (Luke 5.1–9; John 21.5–11). They too took up a new
life that involved proclaiming and witnessing to his coming.

The Samaritan woman's encounter with Jesus seems to have
been healing for her. She is taken seriously, she is known, and
her need for living water is met. Here we see something of a
pattern in the gospel accounts. The way in which female disciples are called seems to entail a kind of therapy of liberation

out of which flows a desire to follow the liberator, rather than a direct command to 'Follow me.' This isn't exclusive to women – we are told that Bartimaeus' discipleship also began in this way (Mark 10.49, 52). Jesus heals women and many of them follow him. On the other hand, it seems clear that some of Jesus' female disciples did not journey with him at all, but remained in their own homes and communities. They were metaphorical rather than literal followers. This may well have been the case for the Samaritan woman, and it seems to have been the case for Martha and Mary of Bethany. Here too women are not unique: the pitifully demonized man who is liberated by Jesus is also told to remain in his own country of the Gerasenes and witness to Jesus there (Mark 5.19).

The women who were healed by Jesus are described as suffering from a range of non-specific health conditions or 'weaknesses', being affected by demons (something we will consider in more detail later in this chapter), fever (Matthew 8.14 and parallels) and curvature of the spine (Luke 13.11).[1] However, the incident that is reported in most detail, and by three out of the four gospel writers, is the healing of the woman with chronic bleeding (Matthew 9.20–22; Mark 5.25–34; Luke 8.43–48). This woman, like her Samaritan sister, also ends up witnessing to Jesus (Luke 8.47), and her story has much to tell us about his healing and liberating encounters that turned people from 'patients' into disciples.

The biblical accounts are not fully explicit about the nature of the woman's trouble (as a child I was told that she was a 'lady with a cut finger'!), and this allows for some interpretative licence. The problem is almost certainly chronic continuous or intermittent bleeding, signifying internal pathology of some kind in either the digestive or the reproductive system. Most commentators have tended to assume the latter: on this reading the woman has very heavy, prolonged, or continuous menstrual periods. This is a reasonable assumption purely because abnormal vaginal bleeding is a very common condition, and this will also be my assumption as I explore the details of her healing encounter with Jesus.

In order to do this I will make use of a model of health conditions that is used widely across the globe: the World Health Organization's International Classification of Functioning, Disability and Health (ICF).[2] Some readers may find the following few paragraphs rather technical. Nevertheless, health conditions are by their nature highly complex, and it is important to use a framework that can do justice to this complexity, and at the same time clarify the key issues. The WHO-ICF model can do just this, and is capable of addressing not only health and illness but also many other aspects of the human situation.

The model states that any given health condition can be expressed at three different levels: *impairment*, *activity limitation*, and *participation restriction*. The meanings of these terms are summarized in Table 2. According to the model, problems at any of these levels occur in, and are affected by, *personal*, *physical* and *social contextual factors*.

To illustrate, the health condition 'multiple sclerosis' may be expressed for an affected individual at the level of *impairment* as degeneration of the fatty material that surrounds the nerves (problem with body structure) and as weakness

Table 2 The WHO-ICF model

Level of description	Meaning	Focus on
Impairment	Problem with structure or function of an organ or body system	Body
Activity limitation	Problem with carrying out meaningful activities of daily life	Behaviour
Participation restriction	Problem with involvement in life situations – social roles and relationships	Social world

and incoordination (problem with body function). It may be expressed at the level of *activity limitation* as a severe difficulty in walking for any distance outside the home. It may be expressed at the level of *participation restriction* as a reduction in employability, with all its associated social disadvantages. *Personal contextual factors* would include the previous illness experience and beliefs of the individual; *physical contextual factors* would include the location and layout of her home; *social contextual factors* would include the attitudes of family, friends and potential employers.

A single health condition can be described simultaneously using any combination of the three levels, and all levels are equally important. Despite what one might think, there is no simple proportional relationship between the different levels of description; a high level of *impairment* doesn't necessarily imply a high level of *activity limitation* and *participation restriction*. This is because individuals vary, health conditions vary and cultures vary. For some conditions (for instance, HIV infection) there can be a microscopic physical *impairment*, no *activity limitation* at all, but major *participation restriction* because of negative social attitudes. Indeed *participation restriction*, often characterized by disempowerment, social exclusion and stigma, may be entirely determined by social attitudes. So, at the level of *participation restriction* the WHO-ICF model can be applied to conditions that are not normally thought of as health-related at all, such as poverty or ethnic origin; its scope therefore includes issues of general human 'well-being'.

The model helps us to see the complex factors that are at work in the life of the woman with chronic bleeding. We begin with her *impairment*, and about this we can only speculate. Perhaps she has uterine fibroids, or some structural damage to her birth canal following childbirth, or perhaps her condition has rendered her 'barren'. She does seem to have experienced pain or discomfort because Mark tells us that she notices a difference in her body when she is healed (Mark 5.29).

We know something more of her *activity limitation*. If she is anaemic (as seems likely) she will have limited stamina. The need to clean herself regularly may interfere with her ability to carry out domestic chores. She is able to walk, at least on this occasion, but she may not be able to walk far or fast. However, she does somehow manage to approach Jesus from behind.

We will gain a better insight into her *participation restriction* when we have considered her personal, physical and social contexts, and they are all important. The woman has a *personal* history. Matthew and Mark speak from the woman's perspective, and give an account of some of her illness beliefs. The woman wants to touch Jesus because she wants to be made well (literally 'saved') and she believes that this will do the job. Her focus on touching Jesus' clothes has often been dismissed as a 'primitive' magical belief by commentators, but personal beliefs in the power of touch have also been shown to be common in the present-day 'developed' West.[3] Mark includes the detail that the woman was a long-term patient[4] under the care of doctors who had, if anything, only made things worse. Luke adds to this that her whole life, or her resources in money, or both, have been spent in the search for a cure. From this we can conclude that she is a woman originally of some means, who has suffered from this condition for 12 years, is probably out of pocket or even in debt, and is desperate for liberation from both the health condition itself and the professional patient role it has forced upon her.

The woman also exists in a *physical context*. It is described clearly by Mark and Luke; she is caught up towards the edges of a pressing crowd. Simple physical access to Jesus is difficult for her, and she approaches from behind. Difficulty in accessing help is a theme in a number of healings. The man by the Sheep-gate pool had given up (John 5.7). Bartimaeus and the Syro-Phoenician woman had to shout their heads off in order to get access to the help they needed. The man who was let down through the roof[5] depended on dedicated friends who were prepared to push through a roof on his behalf (Mark 2.1–12; Luke 5.18–26). This woman acts on her own behalf and pushes through a crowd in a desperate attempt to get the help she needs. All these accounts remind us of something that is globally still true today. Many who have the greatest need of health care have the greatest difficulty in accessing it because it is beyond their geographical and financial reach. They are at the back of a global queue or at the edge of a global crowd.

The woman's *social context* – the attitudes of those around her to a person with this health condition – is perhaps most interesting of all, yet we have little direct information. One important influence may have been the levitical law concerning emission of vital bodily fluids (Leviticus 15.25–31). According to this law the woman is not only unclean in herself, she is also a potential transmitter of pollution to anyone or anything with which the lower half of her body comes in contact. Unlike the situation of the menstruating or *post partum* woman, hers is not a temporary state of affairs. This woman has a chronic condition and, in the terms of the purity laws, is essentially in a permanent state of ritual uncleanness. The levitical sacrifices were a way of marking the transition from unclean to clean when an acute condition had reached its end, for instance after childbirth (Leviticus 12.6–8): Mary and Joseph's visit to the Temple (Luke 2.24) was for this purpose. Chronic conditions of impurity, on the other hand, were not catered for by the sacrificial system. They could only be managed by hygiene: washing and separation of the offensive person from the rest of the community.

This distinction between chronic and acute illness is also marked in our society. Chronic conditions with insidious onset and uncertain course are ambiguous and chaotic. You don't get better from a chronic condition, you learn to live with it. The condition is not just something you have, it becomes incorporated into who you are. Part of the stigma of people with chronic conditions is that they remind the wider community that not everything in life can be fixed.[6] It is no accident that the predominant message on cards sent to people who have fallen sick is 'Get well soon!' This connects with the stories told by people with chronic conditions, who describe a pattern of concerned enquiries of the 'Are you better yet?' sort at the beginning of their illness, followed by awkward avoidance of the subject as the condition persists.

Some chronic conditions are more socially awkward than others. Anything that involves a lack of control of bodily emissions is particularly problematic. This is also reflected in the levitical purity laws, which show a marked concern with control of bodily boundaries, especially eruptions of the skin (Leviticus 12—14) and seepage from reproductive orifices (Leviticus 15). The anthropologist Mary Douglas has argued that blurring of the bodily boundaries of individuals is particularly disturbing for communities whose identity is under threat from those around them, and who are attempting to maintain strong boundaries with their surrounding cultures.[7] Her argument rests on the suggestion that the physical body of the individual symbolizes the corporate community. Permeable bodily boundaries are then seen to symbolize breached community boundaries and loss of community identity and integrity. People with health conditions involving permeable bodily boundaries are therefore psychologically threatening. They are also sources of physical pollution; for their bodily discharges are symbols of the cultural pollution that is the feared result of contact with those outside.

The books of the law probably underwent their final editing at the time of the return from the Babylonian exile, a period when the small nation of Judaea was re-establishing its identity, rebuilding its Temple, and crucially shoring up the boundary walls of its sacred city, as described in the book of Nehemiah.[8] This small nation was being pressed by other cultures (first Persia, then Macedonia, Egypt and Syria) on all sides, and contact – particularly intermarriage with indigenous locals – was being strictly policed (Ezra 9, 10; Nehemiah 13). So, if we accept Douglas' analysis, it is not surprising that in three of the five books of the law (Leviticus, Deuteronomy and Numbers) there is a particular emphasis on bodily purity and pollution regulation.

But did people in rural Galilee nearly five centuries later take any notice of the levitical laws? It is thought that they were generally likely to have been more relaxed than their Judaean counterparts.[9] In addition, sacrificial practice was confined to the Temple in Jerusalem, and a literal interpretation of the purity laws would similarly limit their scope to the Temple precincts. On this understanding the woman would only be an agent of pollution if she were to travel to Jerusalem and attempt to enter the Temple.[10]

On the other hand, there is a concern about purity and holiness running through the gospel accounts expressed in the attitudes of the Pharisees, who are disturbed by Jesus' apparent lack of regard for the keeping of the Sabbath, fasting and ritual hygiene, and his tendency to associate with 'sinners' (Matthew 9.11 and parallels). Indeed as if to emphasize this aspect of his practice, Jesus' encounter with the woman with chronic bleeding is sandwiched between encounters with two other sources of impurity, a demonized man living in a graveyard in Gentile country, and an apparently dead girl.

The Pharisees tried, as it were, to bring the Temple to the people, applying its purity laws in everyday life in a democratic aim to decentralize holiness, so that it found a place in the life of each individual and in local communities.[11] For them, ritual purity was not simply a concern of the Temple and its priestly ministers, it was to be at the core of the daily life of anyone who aspired to personal holiness, no matter where he lived. Mary Douglas also makes the point that the body of the individual, the nation, and the Temple are all bound up together at a symbolic psychological level; the body can be understood as a microcosm of sacred space, specifically the Temple and its sanctuary.[12] It seems likely, then, that even though the Temple was physically over 60 miles away, and even if the levitical purity laws were not anyway rigorously applied by ordinary people in Galilee, attitudes of suspicion, fear and possibly disgust for this woman's health condition would have been in the air alongside attitudes of sympathy.

This mixture of attitudes is not too dissimilar to those of the modern-day West in relation to embarrassing health conditions, of which gynaecological health conditions are a special case. In British culture at least, there is a marked aversion to acknowledging the reality of gynaecological functions, be they healthy or unhealthy. The advertising of female sanitary equipment is marked by euphemism and coyness (blue water to represent menstrual fluid), together with unreality (women in thongs skydiving while having their periods). While words for male genitals and bodily orifices are all terms of offence in the English language, the most offensive swear word by far is the common word for the vagina. Indeed the word 'vagina' is itself used with hesitation in public discourse. In 2003 during the controversy over the appointment of Canon Jeffrey John as bishop of Reading, Bishop Graham Dow remarked that 'It's, well, in a way obvious that the penis belongs with the vagina.'[13] There was a shocked reaction of distaste to his statement by several commentators, crucially not to the simple conservative sentiment it expressed, but to its vocabulary of 'gynaecology'.[14] Nothing more needed to be said to invalidate his point. The introduction of explicit and basic female language into a discourse that until then had been exclusively about males was sufficient to discredit it.

The desire to keep female reproductive organs under strict control and out of public gaze and discourse may arise from an almost sacred respect for their power.[15] When the female reproductive system starts to become unpredictable and to break out of control its power is unleashed and chaos threatens.

Disordered vaginal bleeding is thus dangerous to the community in two ways; it signifies a breach in the boundary of the body politic and it signifies the unleashing of the life force in a chaotic and uncontrollable manner. For this reason it is best to keep the condition hidden and secret. Exposure may entail a sense of shame to all involved.

Taking all of these factors into account, it seems likely that this woman's *participation* in the community was restricted. She would not have been able to enter the Temple and probably other places of worship; it is highly unlikely that she could take part fully in social gatherings or play a full role in her family. As she had spent all she had on being a patient she had lost the resources and time to pursue other life options. *Participation restriction* is often described in the spatial terms of 'social place'. This woman's social place is that of a sick, dirty and depleted person who at the beginning of the story is on the periphery. Her approach to Jesus is from behind, perhaps indicating embarrassment and shame. She is certainly self-conscious: Mark and Luke tell us that she trembles in fear when she is eventually called forward by Jesus. That she touches him at all is a measure of her desperation; that she touches him from behind may be a measure of her fear.

Between them the three gospel accounts tell us that through her act of faith the woman is saved at every level. The *impairment* is removed: the medical sign of impaired function (bleeding) disappears (Mark 5.29; Luke 8.44), and whatever was structurally wrong at the level of body (*sōma*) is healed (Mark 5.29). There is an improved level of *activity* because the woman's behaviour changes. Despite her trembling she is able to come forward and speak (Mark 5.33; Luke 8.47), actions that seem to have been beyond her prior to touching Jesus.

Most fundamentally, there is a dramatic change in social place and *participation*, and this is made clear in all three accounts. The woman moves from the periphery to the centre of the action. Not only that, like Zacchaeus, she is *sought out* and called there by Jesus, where she falls down at his feet in worship. But most important of all, she is addressed by him as 'daughter' (Matthew 9.22; Mark 5.34; Luke 8.48). This is a patriarchal form of address[16] from the head of the family of the people of God to one of its members, from the shepherd to one of his flock, similar to Jesus' assertion that Zacchaeus is a 'son of Abraham'. The woman is thus affirmed as a daughter of the kingdom. She is welcomed into a family and offered both new roles and new relationships.

One of these new roles, according to Luke, is that of a witness who testifies 'to all the people'. No longer is the woman's condition a secret. Presumably having got up from her position of worship, she is able to talk about it: the little detail that she was desperate just to touch Jesus' clothing has been passed down to us because she included it in her story. In Mark's and Luke's versions Jesus' final words summarize what has happened. He tells the woman to 'go in peace'. Luke uses the same word for 'go' – *poreuou* – as that given to the woman taken in adultery: essentially a liberating, 'Get on with your life in peace.'

'Peace' is a weak English translation which does not fully capture all that comes under the umbrella of the Hebrew term *shālôm*. The nearest equivalent we have for it is the notion of 'well-being'. It carries with it a sense of wholeness affecting physical, psychological, or moral domains, and it is always understood as emanating from God.[17] It is relational. The expression, 'Daughter, your faith has saved and continues to save you. Go well on the way' (Luke 8.48) tells us that this woman has been and continues to be made wholly well at every level. This has been her call to a life of discipleship.

But what of Jesus? How has this encounter affected him? We are told that he felt the touch of the woman because he sensed that power had gone out of him. It is usual to understand these words as signifying Jesus' potency as the source of divine power which emanates outwards. But there is another possibility:

the words could refer to a disempowering emptying or *kenosis* (Philippians 2.7). Here *social contextual factors* again become important. According to Leviticus 15.27 the touch of the woman would have polluted Jesus, just as would the touch of lepers and contact with a dead body. Furthermore, he would have become a polluter himself. We start to see that the woman's salvation may have been costly for Jesus. For whatever the precise details of local observance of the purity laws, there is a general thrust to the gospel narratives that Jesus' reputation is tarnished and diminished by his social and physical contact with the wrong sort of people.[18] On this occasion it is the woman who touches Jesus, but he does not resist her touch or censure it, and there are several other instances reported in the Gospels in which Jesus himself initiates physical contact with people who are ritually unclean (e.g. Matthew 8.2–3 and parallels). In some sense Jesus takes on the stigma of polluted people and carries it on his person. There are resonances here with the suffering servant of Isaiah 53 who is referred to by Matthew in the context of Jesus' healing ministry:

> Now as evening came they brought to him many demonized people and he cast out the spirits with a word, and cured all who were ill, in order that what was spoken through Isaiah the prophet might be fulfilled: 'He took our weaknesses and carried our diseases.' (Matthew 8.16–17)

Some scholars have argued that there is more to this than Jesus simply bearing people's burdens. A kind of exchange or 'interchange' may be taking place:[19] people are rehabilitated into the community through Jesus' voluntary self-stigmatization; they are able to participate through his exclusion; they are given life through his death.

There are several indications that something of this sort is indeed happening. First, when Jesus is handed over to the authorities by Judas he moves from being a free agent to being the passive recipient of violent abuse and finally murder at the hands of others. This transition is seen particularly clearly in Mark's Gospel where Jesus is no longer the subject of sentences but becomes instead the object.[20] The Latin root of the word 'passion' is the same as the word for 'patient'. Jesus essentially takes on the patient role, something from which he has freed many, including the woman with chronic bleeding.

Second, the location of Jesus' death is outside the city, beyond the boundary walls. It is Jesus now who is excluded and who inhabits the periphery. The passers-by actually taunt him with this fact – he used to be the powerful one who saved; now he is the weak one and he needs to save himself (Matthew 27.42 and parallels). The writer to the Hebrews (Hebrews 13.12–13) makes the obvious connection that Jesus is now 'outside the camp' – the place designated for polluters (Leviticus 13.46; Deuteronomy 23.10). Expulsion outside the camp is, in the terms of the WHO-ICF model, a formal enactment of exclusion from *participation* in society, with the individual's social position being firmly located on the wrong side of a boundary line.

Finally, Jesus' wounds or stigmata are penetrations of the boundary of his body. He has the marks of the nails in his hands and his feet, and a wound in his side so large that Thomas can put his hand into it (John 20.27). Like the woman – like all women – he bleeds. Jesus' body now marks him as a marginal person, an impure source of pollution. Yet, in his rising from the grave, he 'overcame the power of defilement',[21] and what's more, as the writer to the Hebrews has reminded us, he shifted the centre of gravity of the whole cosmos, so that the periphery has now become its centre.

Jesus takes on the characteristics of those with recognizable physical illnesses, but his stigmatization also extends to accusations of 'having a demon' (John 7.20; 8.48) and of being under the influence of Beelzebul, 'the ruler of demons' (Matthew 9.34; 12.24 and parallels). We are told that several of the women who followed Jesus had been freed from demons, and it is to the call of these women that we now turn.

The seven demons of Mary Magdalene

'There's one little thing I'd like you to think about between now and the next time; what we call "illness" is one of the things men do to women. That may mean something to you or it may not.'

'Oh yes,' said the patient, 'That does mean something to me.'[22]

The Gospels use the phrase 'having a demon' or 'demonized one' (participles of the verb *daimonizomai*), together with the phrase 'having an unclean or evil spirit' to describe certain distressing conditions. (People in the New Testament are never described as being 'possessed by' demons or spirits – they 'have' them in rather the way we might have a cold.) Demonized people are among the crowds who are brought to Jesus for help, and there are several descriptions of his encounters with demonized individuals. In these encounters the presenting problems are lack of speech (Matthew 9.33; 12.22 and parallels); falling about uncontrollably (Matthew 17.15 and parallels); and disturbances of consciousness or sense of identity accompanied by challenging behaviour (Matthew 8.28 and parallels; Mark 1.23–24; Luke 4.33–34). These all conform to a pattern: there is some sort of behavioural disability or disturbance, and there is no obvious physical cause.[23] In terms of the WHO-ICF model there is *activity limitation* without observable structural *impairment*. We should also note that using the literal translation 'demonized' draws attention to the fact that there was likely to be significant *participation restriction* in these conditions, for the demonizing can be done by the community as much as by the identified 'demon'.

So, when the Gospels say that someone has a demon or unclean spirit this is at one level simply an idiom for those

conditions where the focus of concern is the individual's behaviour. But the vocabulary of demons and spirits also reflects
an attempt to *explain* this behaviour. Where there is no clear
physical cause for the problem it is natural to invoke invisible
agents as causes.[24] At the time of Jesus there were many such
agents available in the religious culture, for the writings of the
Second Temple period[25] show evidence of a development of
interest in cosmology and magic, and increasingly elaborate
descriptions of the heavenly and Satanic hosts.[26] While the New
Testament writers are clearly influenced by this, they do not get
involved in the details of demonology, keeping their focus
instead very much on Jesus. They seem to use the term 'demon'
essentially as shorthand for an agent that effects a profound
lack of *shālôm* in the lives of people who do not have an identifiable physical injury or abnormality.

English medical vocabulary still has the legacy of our ancestors' tendency to invoke invisible agents as explanations when
no other could be found, for example 'stroke' (of God) and
'seizure' (by a spirit). With advances in microscopic technology
we are now able to identify structural and functional impair-
ments that account for many of the conditions that may have
baffled people in earlier times. For instance, we now know that
epileptic fits are not the direct work of supernatural agents, but
instead result from abnormal patterns of electrical activity in
brain cells, and that strokes are no more an act of God than any
other medical event, and result from an interruption of the
blood supply to the brain.

In Western society psychological disturbance that causes disability or distress tends to be viewed as a type of sickness, and
it is divided into two sorts: disturbance that has an obvious
cause in the brain, and is the province of neurology; and disturbance that has no single clear cause in the brain, and is
the province of psychiatry. The medical community still has
some hope of further delineating the biological basis of many
psychiatric conditions such as anxiety, depression, mania and

schizophrenia, thus moving them nearer to the province of neurology.[27] However, there remain some conditions that are seen as inherently the province of psychiatry because their origins and essential nature are thought to be psychological and social rather than biological. These are conditions where there is *activity limitation* but no identifiable *impairment* that can account for it and they are the modern West's logical equivalent of demons. In the current Diagnostic and Statistical Manual (DSM-IV)[28] of the American Psychiatric Association (APA) they are grouped under the classes of *somatoform* and *dissociative* disorders. Where many world cultures of the past and present would say a person has a demon, modern Western culture makes a psychiatric diagnosis. In both cases the community is bringing its dominant world view into play in a systematic attempt to make sense of human behaviour that is both deeply troubling and mysterious.[29]

I certainly do not want to take the colonialist position that the modern Western view is the best and that all people having demons are 'really' mentally ill, but I do want to pursue the categories of somatoform and dissociative disorders a little further because these may have some useful light to shed on the situation of the demonized at the time of Jesus.

Somatoform disorders are conditions where an individual presents with severe and genuine *physical symptoms* (such as pain, fatigue, paralysis or convulsions) that cannot be explained by the presence of a general medical condition, and may be a response to psychological stress.

Dissociative disorders, on the other hand, are marked by a *disruption of consciousness* (problems with memory, identity or perception) in the absence of brain disease, and often seem to occur as a response to psychological trauma. The most well known are dissociative amnesia, where large parts of the individual's past life and identity are forgotten; dissociative fugue, where the individual travels to a new place and is confused about her identity (this may have been what happened to

Agatha Christie during the period she went missing in 1926);[30] and dissociative identity disorder in which there are two or more distinct identities or personality states, and at least two of these recurrently take control of the individual's behaviour.[31]

Somatoform and dissociative disorders are the modern versions of 'hysteria',[32] a term that has its origin in the medicine of ancient Greece and Egypt, and that refers to a condition that was thought to be brought about by the movement of the *hysterium* (uterus) around the body. It was thus by definition an exclusively female disorder. While this ancient concept remained central to European medicine over many centuries, a particularly intense revival of interest developed from about 1870. Feminist commentators have drawn attention to women's increasing and often frustrated aspirations to education and independence in the industrialized societies of this time. They interpret at least some of the psychiatric symptoms displayed by women diagnosed as hysterics in this period as a form of cultural protest, and the focus on hysteria by the male medical profession as a reactive means of social control and repression:

> 'Hysteria' was linked with the essence of the feminine in a number of ways. Its vast, unstable repertoire of emotional and physical symptoms – fits, fainting, vomiting, choking, sobbing, laughing, paralysis – and the rapid passage from one to another suggested the lability and capriciousness traditionally associated with the feminine nature. As Dr Edward J. Tilt noted in his textbook on female diseases, 'mutability is a characteristic of hysteria, because it is characteristic of women – "*La donna è mobile*".'[33]

At the turn of the twentieth century Josef Breuer and Sigmund Freud made significant advances in this area by developing a theoretical and therapeutic approach that made a genuine attempt to engage with the psychology of hysterical patients, a group that was by then recognized to include a minority of males.[34] Freud and Breuer's great development was to attempt to understand the *meaning* of the patient's symptoms as expressing the nature of her psychic distress, rather than merely to concentrate on the form that the symptoms took. In his most famous analysis, Breuer suggested that the persistent loss of voice suffered by his young and highly intelligent female patient Anna O was a symbolic representation of her silencing by a stiflingly patriarchal family circle, and her entrapment within the limited role it offered her. Her family refused to allow her a voice, and so her physical voice also ceased to function as a kind of symbolic protest. This understanding of somatoform symptoms – as the only option available for individuals who have become trapped in restrictive family situations – became fairly standard. It is therefore interesting to note this strikingly similar conclusion about demons and spirits based on anthropological observation across a range of cultures:

> . . . spirit-possession, [is something] . . . by means of which women and other depressed categories exert mystical pressures on their superiors in circumstances of deprivation and frustration when few other sanctions are available to them.[35]

Like somatoform symptoms, dissociative symptoms – including the development of multiple identities – arise in individuals who feel trapped, but these individuals may have the additional stress of acute trauma. For instance, their family situations may not just be restrictive, but may also be actively emotionally, physically or sexually abusive.[36] This leads us to wonder whether those individuals in the gospel accounts, whose identities seem to have been taken over by others, and who speak with the voices of others, are examples of subordinate, trapped abused or traumatized individuals. This seems to be a particularly apt question in relation to the demonized man of Gerasa who speaks as if a whole legion of occupying soldiers is inside him. There is no doubting the imagery of rape here. In a challenging reading of this story Peter Horsfield explores the symbolic rape of this man by the demon called Legion:

> The demoniac was a person 'possessed' – literally 'owned' and 'used' – by something beyond himself which ignored or refused to respect his sense of personal boundary and worth and which used him for its own purposes – in this case, as a place to live and as a personal gymnasium.[37]

We can only speculate on this man's history, about which we are told nothing. Suffice it to say that sexual assault on males and females by conquering and occupying forces was common in the ancient world, as it is today.[38]

We know even less about Mary of Magdala. We are told that she had seven demons, an indication of an extremely severe case of demonization, best described as 'total'. In this respect at least she is like the man of Gerasa. It is possible that her condition was similar, and that she experienced herself as inhabited by seven personalities. An alternative possibility is that she had seven disabilities, being unable to feel, hear touch, taste, see, desire and speak.[39] Perhaps she was a survivor of physical or sexual abuse in the domestic or wider sphere. She was certainly not attached to the household of a father, husband or other male relative, being identified instead by her town of origin. This is unique among the gospel women, and it is highly suspicious. Had she been abandoned, or had she run away to escape abuse? What did she have to do in order to survive?

Of course, we have so little evidence that it may seem unwise to speculate. But absence of evidence of abuse should not be mistaken for evidence of absence of abuse. The little information that we do have is muted and oblique, but it is significant and should not be passed over without pause. Indeed it can be argued that it demands speculation, and suspicious speculation at that for, as Elisabeth Schüssler Fiorenza points out, 'biblical texts about women are like the tip of an iceberg, intimating what is submerged'.[40] This insight dawned on me too a few years ago as I surveyed the inscription on a tomb in Dorchester Abbey in Oxfordshire:

> Reader! If thou hast a Heart famed for Tenderness and Pity, Contemplate this Spot. In which are deposited the Remains of a Young Lady, whose artless Beauty, innocence of Mind and gentle Manner once obtain'd her the Love and Esteem of all who knew her. But when Nerves were too delicately spun to bear the rude Shakes and Jostlings which we meet with in this transitory World, Nature gave way. She sunk and died a Martyr to Excessive Sensibility. Mrs SARAH FLETCHER, Wife of Captain FLETCHER, departed this Life at the village of Clifton on the 7 of June 1799 in the 29 year of her age. May her Soul meet that Peace in Heaven which this Earth denied her.

This is a memorial to a young woman who hanged herself from the curtain rail of her bedstead in the house she was visiting, using a pocket handkerchief which she attached to a piece of string. This followed the neglect, probable abuse, and attempt at an advantageous bigamous marriage by her husband. (These circumstances must have influenced the decision to bury her in consecrated ground.) The verdict at the inquest into her death was 'lunacy',[41] and all that we know of her terrible trouble is framed in the understated terms of 'delicately spun nerves' and 'excessive sensibility', phrases that are only intelligible to those in the know. In this light it seems right to ponder on those demons of Mary of Magdala.

What the Gospels (Mark 16.9; Luke 8.2) do tell us beyond doubt is that, unlike Sarah Fletcher, but like the man of Gerasa and the woman with chronic bleeding, Mary of Magdala was made totally well by Jesus. Whatever her demons were, he cast them out. He would have done this with a simple speech-act (Matthew 8.16). The gospel writers agree that Jesus had an astonishing charisma and power in relation to demonized people. Those who were under the control of an alien personality were both attracted and frightened by him. They called out in recognition (unlike the 'normal' people around them) but also in terror at the prospect of being tormented (e.g. Mark 1.24; 3.11). As we saw in Chapter 2, these demonized people were among those who entered into dialogue with Jesus about his identity. They seem to have connected with him in a special sort of way – 'It takes one to know one.' This is surely behind the accusation that Jesus cast out demons by the ruler of demons, and also the observation that on one occasion Jesus' family thought that he was 'out of his mind' (Mark 3.21). It seems likely that he was in the habit of going into visionary trances (Matthew 3.16 and parallels; Luke 10.18).[42] The difference between Jesus and the people he was trying to help was that his trances were healthy and of God's Spirit (Luke 4.18), whereas their disturbances of consciousness were the outcome of dark forces. Yet Jesus was demonized by the authorities for his pains, and in response he warned that to call the Spirit of God Satanic is a sin that cannot be forgiven (Matthew 12.31; Luke 12.10).

Once she was cleansed and healed, Mary, like the man of Gerasa, responded with a desire to keep close to Jesus, and in this case he seems to have acquiesced. While there were friends in Gerasa for the man to return to (Mark 5.19), it may not have been safe for Mary to remain in or return to Magdala. She was, after all, an unprotected and apparently isolated and marginalized woman. She had need of a new family, and this was provided for her by Jesus. Mary remained vulnerable in many ways. On another occasion Jesus talks about the vulnerability of those from whom unclean spirits have been driven out (Matthew 12.43–45; Luke 11.24–26). He makes it clear that driving out a spirit, but leaving the person empty with nothing to replace it, puts her in an even worse position. Better the devil – or the symptoms – that you know. Relinquishing the sick role is of no benefit at all unless there is something positive to take its place.

For Mary, as for many others, this something positive is discipleship. Her cleansing brought with it a call to follow Jesus, to stick close to him at all costs. She had to do this in order to survive physically, psychologically and spiritually. Like the man from Gerasa she must have been profoundly grateful, for she must have felt through Jesus' actions, perhaps for the first time, true love. Jesus loved her back from the twilight zone of the demonized into the human race and the family of the kingdom, just as he loved Jairus' daughter back from *Sheol*. Jesus enabled Mary to get up and become a human being, to arise and become herself. How else could she have received all this but as a call of love?

> My beloved speaks and says to me:
> 'Arise,[43] my love, my fair one,
>   and come away;
> for now the winter is past,
>   the rain is over and gone.
> The flowers appear on the earth;
>   the time of singing has come,
> and the voice of the turtle-dove
>   is heard in our land.
> The fig tree puts forth its figs,
>   and the vines are in blossom;
>   they give forth fragrance.
> Arise, my love, my fair one,
>   and come away.
> (Song of Solomon 2.10–12, NRSV)

7

Jesus teaches

——•◆•——

Rabbouni

Jesus says to her, 'Woman, why are you weeping? Whom are you seeking?' Thinking that he is the gardener, she says to him, 'Sir, if you have removed him, tell me where you have laid him, and I myself will take him away.' Jesus says to her, 'Mary!' Having turned around, she says to him in Aramaic, 'Rabbouni!' (which means Teacher). Jesus says to her, 'Do not hold on to me . . .'   (John 20.15–17a)

As we saw in Chapter 1, Jesus is susceptible to hero worship. If you have been in a place of utter darkness and a wonderful charismatic man lifts you out of it, offering you self-respect and life with a new family, you are likely to form a deep attachment to him. All you want is to be in his arms. This is true now, and it must have been true with many of Jesus' first followers, both men and women. These people adored him. Their grief at his death, their joy at their brief reunion, their sadness at his final departure, and their eagerness for his return all attest to their love for him.[1] In the biblical texts, dominated as they are by the stories of men, we see this most clearly in Peter and Paul.

Like Mary of Magdala, Peter was rescued by Jesus (Matthew 14.30–31) and was passionately devoted to him. He was so attached to Jesus that he followed him all the way into the courtyard of the high priest's house, an amazingly risky thing to do. The wonder is not so much that Peter denies Jesus, but that he follows him as far as he does. It is as if he cannot bear to be apart from Jesus, can think of nowhere else to go (John 6.68a). In the courtyard Peter is drawn to and warms himself over a fire. The Greek word for fire – *phōs* – also means 'light': Peter seems still to yearn for the warmth and light that he has found in Jesus, but must now content himself with something less. In John's account of the meeting between the risen Jesus and Peter on the lakeside, Peter jumps into the water and swims for shore, so eager is he to be close to him again.

Paul too was taken hold of by Jesus (1 Corinthians 15.8; Philippians 3.12) at a time when his life was on a destructive path (Galatians 1.13). Like Peter, and Mary of Magdala, he wanted to hold on to the Christ Jesus who was saving him. His letters are overflowing with an intense affection, gratitude and devotion to Christ that seem at times to have erotic over-tones (for instance, Philippians 3.8–9). However, to describe Paul's attachment to Christ as simply 'erotic' does not really do it justice. Paul is not concerned with the beauty of Christ's person, or of basking in the delights of his touch, a common preoccupation in some later Christian mystical traditions.[2] Paul seems instead to show an awe-struck admiration of Christ's integrity of character and his radical heroic act through which God achieved the salvation of the human race. He also shows a deep and surprised sense of being affirmed as a worthwhile human being, and a desire to identify with his hero. His one reference to a mystical experience of Christ (2 Corinthians 12.2) is not so much about the achievement of an erotic union as the receiving of revealed truth, and this is highly significant.

Peter, Paul and Mary of Magdala can all be said to have had an attachment bond with Jesus, of the sort that babies and young children develop for their primary caregivers, usually their parents.[3] As we have seen, they all wanted to stay close to Jesus and indeed to hold on to and be held by him. In their dif-ferent ways they needed to be cared for by him, and they all knew – perhaps Mary most of all – that they could only survive by remaining attached to Jesus. This is in a sense eternally true for us all (John 15.5).

Yet the aspects of the relationship with Jesus that draw the disciple in, meeting the need to be saved, seen, known, called – indeed loved and protected under the wings of the caregiver – and the complex rush of affectionate feelings that goes with all of these, begin, with time, to find their place as parts of a more broadly based relationship:

> . . . the nature of a relationship between two individuals grows out of the total history of their interactions. These interactions are likely to be varied, involving a number of categories of content . . . For example, a mother may interact with her infant as caregiver, as playmate, and/or teacher. All these facets characterize that particular relationship, but perhaps only one of them – the caregiving component – is directly related to the protective function . . . [of] attachment.[4]

In this way, we find that Jesus is not forever in a relationship with his disciples where there is lots of kissing and cuddling going on. Mutual affectionate outpouring may mark the beginning of the relationship (Luke 15.20)[5] and re-emerge when separation looms (John 13; see also Acts 20.37–38 for a lovely human parallel), but as the relationship develops, other factors come into play. The reason that Peter cannot leave Jesus is that he has 'the *words* (*rhēmata*) of Eternal Life' (John 6.68b). Paul is caught up in a heavenly experience of Christ and hears 'inexpressible words (*rhēmata*) that a human being may not speak' (2 Corinthians 12.4). The relationship is not just about affectionate caregiving and receiving, important as this is; it's about the disclosure of information concerning matters of substance. Immediately after his discourse on the true vine and the importance of attachment, Jesus goes on to say to his disciples, 'I no longer call you servants, for the servant does not know what his master is doing; but I have called you friends, for all that I have heard from my Father I have made known to you' (John 15.15).

Going deeper into Christ entails a raising of status, indeed an increase in power, because to hold information is to hold power. The disciple is indeed the beloved little child, but he is also the pupil – *she* is also the pupil, for *Mary* calls Jesus 'teacher', and she too is given *rhēmata* (Luke 24.11).

The meeting of Jesus and Mary as described in chapter 20 of John's Gospel is often treated as the ultimate romantic depiction of a reunion of two lovers parted under tragic circumstances. Mary has twice lost the man she loves – first to violent death and then, she presumes, to grave-robbers. She is desperately searching for him in the garden, and weeping as she does so. She at least wants to minister to his body with the myrrh and aloes set aside for the purpose by Nicodemus (John 19.39–40), yet she cannot find it:

> Where has your beloved gone,
> O fairest among women?
> Which way has your beloved turned,
>   that we may seek him with you?
>
> My beloved has gone down to his garden,
>   to the beds of spices,
> to pasture his flock in the gardens,
>   and to gather lilies.
>
> Upon my bed at night
> I sought him whom my soul loves;
> I sought him, but found him not;
>   I called him, but he gave no answer.
> 'I will rise now and go about the city,
>   in the streets and in the squares;
> I will seek him whom my soul loves.'
>   I sought him, but found him not.
> The sentinels found me,
>   as they went about in the city.
> 'Have you seen him whom my soul loves?'

113

Scarcely had I passed them,
    when I found him whom my soul loves.
I held him, and would not let him go . . .
    (Song of Solomon 6.1–2; 3.1–4, NRSV)

As she weeps, Mary encounters a stranger who calls her by name with an astonishing intimacy, so that she recognizes her love and immediately tries to hold him. It is a breathtakingly erotic moment, heightened by Mary's tears and Jesus' quiet approach from behind. Yet she doesn't cry out 'My love!' or some Aramaic equivalent of 'Darling!' She does not call out the name of Jesus. Oddly, she says, 'Teacher!'

Mary of Magdala loves Jesus *and* she is his disciple – his follower and his pupil. Indeed her love is part of her discipleship, as it is for Peter and Paul.

The New Testament tells us of another Mary who is Jesus' pupil. This is Mary of Bethany, who seats herself at Jesus' feet in order to listen to his words (Luke 10.39), rather as Jesus before her sat among the rabbis in the Temple.[6] Before Jesus was a rabbi he too was a pupil. (Luke uses the same turn of phrase – 'seated listening' – to describe the attitude of the young Jesus and Mary.) Mary's sister Martha was also a disciple of Jesus. Like all good disciples, Martha had 'received' Jesus (Matthew 18.5; Luke 9.48) into her life and into her home (Luke 10.38). Martha expresses a particular view of discipleship: receiving Jesus means engaging in service. She is correct. Later in Luke's Gospel Jesus says:

'The kings of the Gentiles lord it over them; and those having power over them are called "benefactors". But not so with you; rather the greatest among you must become as the youngest, and he who leads as he who serves. For who is greater, he who reclines at table or he who serves? Is it not he who reclines at table? But I am in your midst as one who serves.'

(Luke 22.25–27)

Martha's diaconal activities – administering the practicalities of the household into which Jesus and perhaps others have been invited – are a type of servant leadership; they are central to her piety, and she is preoccupied with them.[7] Not only that, she seems to be irritated by the seemingly passive and self-indulgent behaviour of her sister. But Jesus points out to Martha that 'receiving' does not just mean welcoming, it also means hearing: 'Are you receiving me?'

In this vein, Henri Nouwen has described listening as hospitality:

> Listening is paying full attention to others and welcoming them into our very beings . . . Listening is a form of spiritual hospitality by which you invite strangers to become friends.[8]

The disciple is required to study and learn as much as she is required to serve, in fact more so because the choice Mary has made is 'better' (Luke 10.42).

'Servant leadership' is a popular theme in church circles these days.[9] But it is a model of discipleship that should be handled with discernment and care because it is not indiscriminately applicable. It is rarely noted that wherever in the Gospels Jesus emphasizes his role as a servant, and calls his followers to emulate it, he is specifically addressing *men*.

The exhortation to a servant attitude is a good example of male discourse that is readily received by women as applying to themselves. At the very beginning of this book there was another example: Thérèse Martin's appropriation of the male call narratives as part of her own experience of discipleship. Those who oppose women's aspiration to leadership positions in the Church often assert that the Gospels contain no instances of Jesus calling a woman to follow him, and that women's appropriation of such call narratives is unwarranted. It is ironic that the same argument is not applied to Jesus' call to servanthood, a call that is never addressed to a woman in the Gospels. Instead we have Jesus' comment to Martha that her preoccupation with 'much serving' (*pollēn diaconian*) has diverted her from the better path of sitting at the feet of her teacher.

Jesus' teaching on servanthood often arises in response to male rivalry:[10] James and John ask for preferment in the kingdom (Matthew 20.20ff.; Mark 10.35ff.); the Twelve argue among themselves on the road about who is the greatest (Mark 9.33ff.); the apostles[11] argue about who is the greatest at the last supper (Luke 22.24ff.). Even when the teaching is not a direct response to male rivalry, it occurs in 'male only' contexts (Matthew 23.11;[12] Luke 17.5–10; John 13.3ff.). It is addressing a pattern of behaviour that, in modern Western society at least, has been found to be more characteristic of men than of women:

> Assertiveness tends to have different contours in men compared with women. Men generally assert themselves in a forceful or controlling manner, and women more often in a manner that acknowledges the rights of others as well as their own rights . . . Assertive behaviour that promotes oneself over others is more typical of men. Men seem to prefer to assert themselves in hierarchical relationships more than women do . . . The greater attraction of men than women to social hierarchies also emerges in men's greater social *dominance.*[13]

In his teaching of kingdom values Jesus is turning the habitual tendencies of his male followers on their heads. In his dealing with Martha he seems to be doing a similar thing with a female habitual tendency; for 'serving' seems to come more easily to women (Matthew 8.15 and parallels): 'Women also often express their dominance and assertiveness through group-oriented behaviors that facilitate the work of others.'[14]

Jesus seems to be saying that those for whom servanthood does not come naturally, either because of their temperament or because of their social position, need to become much more like servants. Those for whom servanthood has become a preoccupation that diverts them from God's call need to down tools and listen. This call to a freedom from habitual ways of being in the world is one of the things that raises both men and women up above themselves. As many, many feminist commentators have argued,[15] the application of a servant model to groups that are already disempowered and exploited by their masters is simply oppression with a pseudo-Christian gloss – a wolf in sheep's clothing. After all, the words of Mary of Nazareth assure us that God does not behave like that: 'He has taken down the rulers from their thrones, and raised up those of low status' (Luke 1.52).

Jesus transformed the lives of women like Mary of Magdala by, among other things, offering them the opportunity of access to his teaching as they followed him on the road and, as in the case of Martha and Mary of Bethany, in the privacy and safety of their homes. His lifestyle of travelling from place to place and then accepting hospitality in people's homes (Matthew 8.20; 10.14 and parallels) made his teaching accessible to women in a way that would not have been possible for them had he confined himself to public spaces or exclusively male domains.[16] Not only that, the content of Jesus' teaching is full of the concerns of women and is located in the world of women. It is not merely that women were fortunate to be in the domestic vicinity and could eavesdrop on the men's business of teaching: the teaching was directed at women as much as it was directed at men. The everyday life of women is transfigured through the teaching of Jesus, just as the lives of his female followers were transformed. The fact that women are invited to be his pupils is a measure of the transformation he has wrought in their lives, but the teaching is also itself the agent of transformation.

The most dramatic instance of this is provided by Luke's account of a meeting between Jesus and a woman in a private home (Luke 7.36ff.). Jesus has been invited to the house of Simon the Pharisee – an indication that the relationship between Jesus and the Pharisees was not simply one of mutual hostility.[17] Suddenly a woman enters the house bringing with her a jar of perfumed ointment. She weeps over Jesus' feet and dries them with her hair, then she rubs the ointment into them, kissing them all the while.

When I first heard this story as a child I found it disgusting. When I was about 11 years old I expressed this feeling to a teacher at my school. I was slightly surprised when she said that she agreed with me. This gave me the courage to expand on my feelings. It was the idea of using your own hair to clean a man's dirty feet that made me shudder and cringe. My teacher was outraged. 'Don't you realize,' she exclaimed, 'that our Lord's feet would have been clean – the story is disgusting because his pure body was touched by the dirty hair of a dirty woman!'

While we had diametrically different perspectives on this story we shared an emotion, one of disgust and unease. This is understandable because Luke's account is deeply, deeply disturbing. It's disturbing because of the extended physical contact between Jesus and the woman. It's disturbing because of the nature of this contact, heavy with sexual overtones. It's disturbing because of the uninhibited and uncontrolled emotion of the woman. It's disturbing because of Jesus' contrasting passivity and evident enjoyment of her ministrations.

We are told little about the woman other than she is 'sinful' and happens to be in town, either because she lives there or is visiting. It is therefore extremely unlikely that she has been invited to the house of a Pharisee. She obtains an alabaster jar of ointment, which would have been expensive, so she is presumably wealthy. We are not told whether her hair is already loose or if she unveils herself and then lets down her hair only once she is in the house. While loose hair may have been a shameful sign in adult married women in later Jewish circles, its significance at the time of Jesus is uncertain.[18] Anyway, it is clear that the woman cannot be identified as 'sinful' from her appearance alone because Simon reflects that it would take a prophet to discern this (Luke 7.39). What the woman then goes on to do with hair, hands, and mouth is, however, right on the edge of acceptable public behaviour.

She pays great attention to Jesus' feet. In ancient Greek and Roman culture, and at points in the Hebrew Bible, a man's feet are presented as a focus of his sexuality.[19] This is evident, for instance, in the story of Ruth and Boaz (Ruth 3.4–8). So the woman's actions would have troubled Luke's first readers, as they trouble Simon the Pharisee in the story. Like all sexual overtures apart from the most rapacious, what this woman does is ambiguous, open to multiple interpretations. Perhaps it is a type of worship. After all, people did throw themselves at Jesus' feet when they wanted help (e.g. Mark 5.22) or when overcome with awe and wonder (Matthew 28.9). Perhaps it is an attempt at domestic service, rather like the offering of hot towels by air cabin staff. Because Jesus does not appear to flinch or withdraw from her attentions, Simon concludes that he has misread the situation as harmless when it is in fact full of danger. (There is a precise parallel here in the story of the prodigal son: the older brother sees fit to remind his father that the son he is embracing is unclean (Luke 15.30).) If Jesus had understood 'what sort of woman' she is he would understand what sort of overture this is – and anyway, her kisses should have given the game away. This leads us to the conclusion that the woman's previous sinful life has involved sexual sin of some sort.

Jesus counteracts Simon's objections first by demonstrating that he is a prophet: he knows Simon's thoughts even though they remain unspoken, and he talks about the woman's many sins (Luke 7.47), indicating that he knows the woman perfectly well, just as he knew the woman of Samaria. What he has to say on the subject is introduced by Simon's words, 'Teacher, speak!' (Luke 7.40). It is therefore a solemn pronouncement. Jesus goes on to tell a short parable which is highly psychological in nature. This woman's behaviour seems to be over the top and out of control. There is too much of it and it is too emotionally and erotically intense for comfort. Jesus says, as we saw in Chapter 1, that her behaviour need not be a cause for concern because it is simply commensurate with the forgiveness she has received and continues to receive for her sins: 'And having turned towards the woman, he said to Simon, "Do you see this woman? . . . her cancelled sins were many since she loves so much"' (Luke 7.44a, 47–48a).

Crucially, Jesus reframes the woman's behaviour as an act of Christian love (*agapē*). He goes into some detail; the woman has, like Martha, received him with the host's kiss of welcome and provision of water for his feet (Genesis 18.4). She has also anointed Jesus in recognition of his kingly status. This all marks out the woman as a disciple – one who not only receives Jesus but who also understands his identity as the Messiah. Of course, she hasn't done any of this in a literal sense. She has done what comes naturally to her. Jesus does not negate this. He does not turn her *eros* into *agapē* and her emotionalism into piety. He says her *eros* and her emotionalism are the gifts that she brings with her into her life of discipleship. Her *agapē* incorporates her *eros* and her piety incorporates her emotionalism.

Finally he addresses the woman herself. And he says something that by now should sound familiar: 'Your faith has saved and continues to save you. Go well on the way' (Luke 7.50). If this woman is to go well on the way she must get up from the floor and start walking. Perhaps she goes home. Perhaps she waits outside for Jesus to leave, and follows him on his journey. Whatever she does, she has been raised up, not just in relation to her low position on the floor, but in relation to the male householder Simon. Jesus contrasts the two of them point by point. Everything that the woman has done indicates her reception of Jesus. Everything that Simon has omitted, including giving Jesus credit for some intelligence, has shown that the host of the reception has not actually received his guest at all.

Jesus' reaction to the overture of this woman is not simply that of a detached analyst. In his words of rebuke to Simon for his neglect of his duties as a host there seems to be a trace of the hurt evident in the lament over Jerusalem. Jesus would have liked to be welcomed with a kiss, offered water for his dusty feet, and recognized by anointing with oil. These are not just proper behaviours, Jesus would have *liked* them. So he seems grateful for the affection and deference of this woman, albeit overblown. He was also a flesh and blood man who must have enjoyed sensual touch as much as he enjoyed the beauty of the lilies of the fields (Matthew 6.28–29), the company of friends, and good food and drink (Matthew 11.19). The woman's womanly gift has been genuinely appreciated. There has been something of a two-way transaction at work.

The woman is an exemplary disciple. She is held up, raised up, as a model for others to emulate. And she is not the only woman who has this honour conferred on her by Jesus.

Women's work

Sharon had no chocolate, no alcohol and she was completely hormonal. Still, if she could find a man to nag, then maybe the day could still be salvaged.[20]

In the English language there are several single-syllable pejorative terms for women that end with the sound 'ag'. These variously denigrate older women, women of 'easy virtue' and ugly women. The word 'nag' is used to denote a persistent querulous goading of others – stereotypically a hen-pecked husband – into action. Nagging, or – as teachers and occupational therapists often refer to it – 'verbal prompting', seems to be part of the work of women. This is perhaps because they often have the understanding to know what must be done but lack the physical strength or social position to effect it. They must instead rely on more powerful others such as husbands or sons. Jesus' words to his mother at the wedding of

Cana could be interpreted as 'Stop your nagging, woman!' However, as we have already seen, Mary's verbal prompt to her son is vindicated by his subsequent actions.

This transformation of nagging is seen even more clearly in Jesus' parable of the persistent widow:

> 'In a certain city there was a judge, neither fearing God nor respecting people. Now in that city there was also a widow who kept coming to him saying, "Vindicate me against my opponent." And for some time he would not. But after this he said to himself, "Though I do not fear God nor respect people, because this widow keeps bothering me I will obtain justice for her, so that she doesn't in the end wear me out with her continual visits." ' And the Lord said, 'Listen to what the unrighteous judge says. And will not God grant justice to his chosen ones who cry to him day and night? Will he be slow with them? I say to you he will act speedily to accomplish justice for them.'
>
> (Luke 18.2–8a)

Jesus holds up this woman's relentless bothersome behaviour as virtuous, and a model for prayer. The woman is a widow and therefore at the bottom of the pile; the man is a powerful judge. All she can do is to nag him, and it turns out to be highly effective, like the dripping of a tap that wears away the stone beneath it. The Christian disciple may not be able to do much, may only be able to take small steps, but this is no reason to give up. God may not answer prayer immediately, but this is no reason to give up praying nor to give up hoping. Like the mustard seed (Matthew 13.31–32 and parallels), the Christian disciple may be tiny, but her small size belies her potential productivity.

As I write this, a just settlement policy for Gurkha soldiers and their families has been obtained in large part through the relentless nagging of UK government officials by one bothersome woman,[21] a strikingly close parallel with the story of the persistent widow and the unrighteous judge. Perhaps it is the perseverance of women in the face of adversity that made them particularly fit to be the first witnesses to the raising of Jesus, something we will examine in more detail in the next chapter.

Of course, it is somewhat flippant to talk of 'nagging' as the work of women. Women's work is primarily hard physical labour, often combined with childbearing and childcare. In most traditional societies looking after the home, cooking and washing (and hence fetching water), and growing herbs and vegetables form the core of women's work. Women may also be involved in commercial activities through cottage industries such as weaving or spinning. They may often be required to assist men working on the land, sometimes carrying out the major part of this work.

Jesus' teaching makes reference to the traditional work of women in the eastern Mediterranean world of his time, alongside the traditional work of men. As we noted in Chapter 3, gender pairs appear from time to time. In one block of teaching in which he is exhorting his disciples not to worry, Jesus talks about birds (Matthew 6.26; Luke 12.24). His point is that these creatures do not work the land for their food, yet nevertheless they are provided for. He is addressing those, mainly men, whose responsibility it is to provide grain for themselves, their families and their communities and who could worry themselves sick about their crops. Yet Jesus doesn't stop there. The second part of his lesson concerns the lilies of the field (Matthew 6.28; Luke 12.27). Here he is addressing women whose responsibility it is to provide clothing for themselves and their families, and perhaps to earn some money as well. These are women who 'toil and spin'. The distinctive concerns of women who must work and provide are woven into his teaching.

The contexts in both Gospels (Matthew 5.1; Luke 12.22) make it clear that Jesus is talking to his disciples. He is not minimizing the desperate need of the crowds on whom he has shown so much compassion. He is encouraging those who have received him and wish to follow him to shift their focus so that they no longer worry about the typical concerns of daily life but instead see the bigger picture that is the kingdom. In doing this he uses examples from the world of work of both men and women. (In true patriarchal style the male example always comes first.) This is another indication, if it were needed, that the group of Jesus' disciples was made up of both women and men.

A further, and amusing, example of the work of men and women is given in Jesus' discourse on the coming of the Son of Man (Matthew 24.40–41; Luke 17.34–35). Here he says that two men will be going about their regular activities, and that one will be taken and the other left; two women will be going about their regular activities, one will be taken and the other left. In the final judgement where the sheep are separated from the goats, the wheat from the tares, women and men will be found in both categories. The second coming will be so sudden that they will be engaged in their everyday pursuits, and thus taken by surprise. For women this activity is grinding meal. In Matthew's version the men are in a field, perhaps working. In Luke's version, which is probably closer to the original source,[22] the men are on a couch, relaxing or sleeping because that is what men do. In both versions their female counterparts are most definitely toiling because that is what women do. There seems to be a nice piece of social observation going on here.[23]

Jesus also uses the work of men and women as a picture of the kingdom itself. The kingdom of God is like a mustard seed sown by someone, which grows to an unexpectedly enormous size (Matthew 13.31–32 and parallels). Its growing is hidden, secret and mysterious. It is also like yeast that a woman mixed into flour until it rose (Matthew 13.33; Luke 13.21). Its growing, too, is hidden, secret and mysterious. It is interesting that the seed grows itself by thrusting upwards above the earth that nurtures it. On the other hand, the yeast acts by facilitating the growth of that with which it comes in contact. Both sorts of growth are good. Both have something to tell us about the kingdom. Each in its way resonates with the two different styles of assertiveness, one more characteristic of males, one more characteristic of females, described earlier in this chapter.

Whenever I bake bread or watch over the germination of seeds I have planted I cannot help but think of these lessons of Jesus. This was surely his intention: to instil in the minds of his male and female hearers images that would be evoked again and again as they went about their daily lives in the home and the fields. The fact that the work of human hands provides superb material for Jesus' teaching about the kingdom affirms the potential dignity of human labour. It raises it up. Planting seeds and baking bread are actions that cooperate with the creativity of God. When Adam and Eve (the first gender pair) are expelled from the Garden of Eden they enter the adult world of sex and work (Genesis 3.16, 19), two things from which we aim to protect our children. But they have not grown up in any positive sense: for the woman sex is tainted by subservience to the rule of her husband, for the man work has become a thankless grind. This was true for many people at the time of Jesus as it is now. Yet his teaching on seeds and yeast points to glimmers of hope in the world of work – little places where things can be different. And his teaching about the woman who anoints his feet affirms that sex can be a delightful and sacred gift rather than a profane means of enforcing servitude.

A final gender pair is found only in Luke's Gospel. This is the shepherd who searches for his lost sheep and the woman who searches for her lost coin (Luke 15.3–10). As with all the other gender pairs, the male version is told first.[24] There is a story of a wealthy man who takes on the job of shepherd[25] in order to seek and save a single lost sheep from a flock of 100. This is followed by the story of a woman who searches diligently for a single coin out of a collection of ten.

The woman in the parable of the lost coin is depicted as an active and responsible keeper of resources. These resources would have supported her family or perhaps her business. In Acts, Luke presents some examples of eastern Mediterranean businesswomen (Tabitha in Acts 9.39; Lydia in Acts 16.14), who had extended essentially domestic activities such as weaving into commercial ventures.[26]

In family finances every penny counts. In the same way, says Jesus, in the kingdom of God every person counts. Every person is worth God's seeking and saving. This includes the marginal folk who were drawing near to Jesus and who formed the focus of an attack by his critics (Luke 15.1). And who stands for God – for Jesus – in this parable? It is a *woman*. Jesus, as it were, says, 'I am like a housekeeper – a small businesswoman.' As we have already seen, he says, 'I am like a mother hen.' He says, 'The concern I have for you, that God has for you, is like your concern for your children, like your concern for your household and finances. It is a deep concern to protect and to care. It is a concern to make things whole and complete.'

When Jesus teaches about women or to women he doesn't say how beautiful and pure they are. He doesn't expound on the temptation they might pose to high-minded young men. On the contrary, he says that when a man sees a woman as a sexual object *he* is committing a sin against her (Matthew 5.28), and insists that a woman cannot just be thrown away when a man tires of her (Matthew 5.32 and parallels). He notes but doesn't denigrate women's habit of 'verbal prompting', instead using it as a model for spiritual persistence. On several occasions he compares women favourably to men. Above all, he takes for granted the fact that women's lives are full of work – domestic, commercial, administrative and educational, and he connects strongly with this because he too is a worker.

The kingdom of God is seen to inhabit and transform the world of human work, so much so that God is said to be like a working shepherd or housewife. But the work of *women* is particularly important, if not vital. For Jesus' earthly ministry depended on it and, as we shall see, there is a sense in which his resurrection could not have happened without it.

8

Jesus entrusts

———•◦•◦•———

From their own resources

What can I give him,
Poor as I am?
If I were a shepherd
I would bring a lamb,
If I were a wise man
I would do my part,
But what I can I give him –
Give my heart.[1]

All four Gospels have a version of the story of the woman who anointed Jesus. They vary quite a lot in their details, including which part of his body was involved, but there is also quite a lot of overlap, and this cannot be simply accounted for by systematic differences between the sources the four writers were using. It was perhaps a notorious story that was repeated and argued about in several quarters. The basic message of the story is, however, the same in all the Gospels. A woman anoints Jesus in a private house, those present criticize her, and Jesus defends her. In Mark's version Jesus says this: 'Let her be; why do you trouble her? She has carried out a fitting action on me . . . She has done what she could; she has anointed my body ahead of time in preparation for burial' (Mark 14.6, 8).

This is the same message that we find in Luke. The woman brings herself, her own resources. She does what she can. As in

Luke's version, she is raised up, but the emphasis is somewhat different. The woman is credited with having the insight that Jesus' death is approaching; her response is interpreted as an anticipatory funeral ritual. She cannot prevent his death, but in a small way she decides to do something that might make a difference to his passing. Jesus goes on to say that her actions will always be recounted wherever the gospel is preached. As in Luke's version, we get the impression that Jesus deeply appreciates what she has done, extravagant and pointless as it may seem.

We return here to the odd notion that Jesus seems to need people. We saw in Chapter 2 that Jesus' identity is negotiated with a host of other folk, realized through encounters with men and women. John's account of the meeting between Jesus and the Samaritan woman begins by telling us that Jesus was 'worn out from the journey'. The first thing that he does when he sees the Samaritan woman is to ask her for a drink. In Chapter 5 we saw that there is an irony to this request, for it is the woman who has a deep spiritual thirst. Nevertheless, Jesus the man is tired, dusty and thirsty. He has no bucket, and he needs the help of this woman.

At other points Jesus seems to have more of a psychological than a physical need of people. He needs the love of the woman who anoints him. He needs the companionship of his friends on the night that he is handed over. He says to them, 'I have eagerly desired to eat this Passover with you before I suffer' (Luke 22.15, NRSV). Eating Passover together is a bit like having your Christmas dinner together. It is the ultimate mark of family solidarity and connection. Jesus wanted, indeed seemed to need, this connection with his friends. As he prayed in great agony to his Father in the garden he wanted his friends nearby. It wasn't that he thought they could prevent his arrest; later when they tried to do this he stopped them. He just wanted, needed, them close by: 'So, could you not stay awake with me one hour?' (Matthew 26.40, NRSV).

In several ways Jesus used the resources of his followers to support his ministry. When he calls Peter he welcomes his skill as a fisherman which, he says, will be put to good uses as he catches people (Matthew 4.19; Mark 1.17). It is sometimes remarked that Jesus' disciples were a motley crew whose key players were 'simple fishermen'. In fact fishermen would have had precisely the sophisticated skills that Jesus needed. They were used to pulling together as a team in the most adverse of circumstances; good communication, cooperative working and an eye for danger and opportunity are all vital if you are to return in one piece from a storm on Lake Galilee. At one point in his ministry we are told that Jesus asked his fishermen disciples to fetch him a boat so that he could escape from the crowds who were pressing upon him on the lake shore (Mark 3.9), which they proceeded to do. There was a risk that Jesus would be crushed by the weight of human need that he was bearing, and he in his turn had his own need for his disciples to help him manage the situation.

The most fundamental expression of Jesus' need for humans to do what they can comes in the story of the feeding of the multitudes. The bread provided by Jesus is in some respects like the manna provided by the Lord for the people of Israel who were starving as they wandered in the desert (Exodus 16). But it is also different. For this bread does not appear as if from nowhere; it is instead a transformation of what the people have brought themselves. Jesus changes it into something much greater, beyond their wildest dreams (Matthew 14.16–18 and parallels). The people bring what they can, and it is very little indeed. But Jesus wants this, seems to need this, to work on. He cannot work with nothing. He cannot do great works where there is no human faith (Mark 6.3–5).

In the Gospels when Jesus heals or saves people he does not say, 'The Lord has saved you.' He says, '*Your faith* has saved you.' In an economy of grace this may seem an anomalous statement. Surely it is God who is at work? Surely, 'We are not worthy so much as to gather up the crumbs under thy table'?[2] Surely, 'Nothing in my hand I bring, simply to thy cross I cling'?[3]

Yet the Syro-Phoenician woman says, 'I *am* worthy to gather the crumbs!' and Jesus says, 'Yes, you are! Thanks for that insight.' A young boy says, 'I've got five loaves and a couple of fishes in my hand; are they any use?' and Jesus takes them and does wonders.

There is a pattern to the relationship between God and humanity. God watches and waits. At some point, often at times of great distress,[4] human beings turn God-wards, bringing with them their small talents, their fleeting insights, their desperate needs, their meagre rations. God then acts. But he doesn't just meet them halfway; he acts disproportionately in a pre-emptive act of love and compassion that is massively greater than anything that they are able to bring to the encounter (Luke 15.20; Romans 5.8). Then they in their turn respond in acts of love, and find themselves able to do more than they had ever thought (Luke 19.8). So, the works of the Christian disciple – the continual transformative bringing back of what she has to God – are the expression of, not the condition for, the love that she has received. The Christian works out her salvation (Philippians 2.12), but this does not mean that she has earned it (Ephesians 2.8–9).

Nevertheless, *something* is required of her in this process. Perhaps it is a kind of permission. God watches, waits and, like the mother hen, he yearns and sometimes calls. But he will only act if there is some sign of human consent, some human cooperation. *He has chosen to need rather than to command.* This is the grace of the incarnation where, in entering the created order, God entrusts himself to human beings. It is also adult-to-adult behaviour. The prodigal son goes away a child, but in letting him go (rather than commanding him to stay or throwing him out) his father has chosen to treat him like an adult, painfully embracing all the needy vulnerability that this entails. The father has entrusted himself to his son. The realization of the son's adult status begins as he decides to turn homewards, a small act of faith that is nevertheless marked by those significant words, 'I will get up' (Luke 15.18a). The father's risky act of trust has been vindicated.

As we have seen, the Son of Humankind also entrusted himself to human beings. In Luke's Gospel we are told of a particular contribution made by women to the needs of Jesus and his disciples, and therefore to his divine mission (Luke 8.3). Luke says that certain women 'provided for them[5] from their own resources'. The interpretation of Luke 8.1–3, a single very long and therefore ambiguous sentence (see page 88), in which these words occur, is hotly contested in New Testament scholarship. The debate focuses on the following questions. Who does 'they' refer to? Is it Mary of Magdala, Joanna, Susanna, or the 'other' women, or all of these? Whoever 'they' are, who is 'them'? Is it Jesus, Jesus and the Twelve, Jesus and all the male disciples, or the whole company including the women themselves? What does 'provided for' mean? Does it mean domestic chores, administrative duties, or financial support? What does 'own resources' mean? Does it mean 'they' did the housework themselves, or that some – perhaps Joanna – were wealthy patrons, or that 'they' could earn money through cottage industries to support the group? Were 'they' too busy 'providing' to take any active part in proclaiming the kingdom or did they multi-task?

It is tempting to ask one further question: Who cares? However, there is a good reason why this text is so hotly debated: it has been seen by many as offering a pattern for gender-specific roles in the Church. People have a tendency to search the Scriptures for prescriptive templates on which to base current church organization, and so knowing what this text 'really means' is seen to be important. If you have an axe to grind this looks like a good text on which to do so, for within it you could potentially find support for women bishops or the exclusion of women from all significant ministries in the Church. But this text is not something on which to grind an axe; it will not bear it, and it should not be made to do so. We have to learn to live with its ambiguity and to treat it with some respect.

The simplest way to understand the text is that a large group of women was among the disciples who followed Jesus in his Galilean ministry. It contained some prominent individuals. Just as Peter, James and John were prominent among the Twelve, Mary of Magdala was prominent among the women (and Joanna seems to have been known to Luke or his sources, and also possibly to Paul).[6] Some or all members of this group contributed[7] to the common purse that was kept by Judas (John 12.6; 13.29), and served the group in other ways. The most natural conclusion is that this refers to the whole group, including the women themselves. (If I say that I know a man who lives with his girlfriend and their daughter and that he 'provides for them', the natural conclusion is that this refers to provision for the family unit including himself. If I say that his girlfriend 'cooks their tea' when he gets in from work, it is natural to conclude that she cooks a meal for the whole family unit including herself.)

What is important about this text is that it reminds us that women followed Jesus from the beginning of his ministry in Galilee, something that Mark also emphasizes in his Gospel (Mark 15.41; followed by Matthew 27.55), and with less ambiguity than Luke. Mark says that the women served Jesus only, and there is no indication of money. Mark's use of the term 'serve' (*diakonein*) is less domestic and administrative than Luke's and seems to refer more to the kind of ministerial service a pupil owed his teacher.[8] But whatever their ministrations, we can conclude that Jesus needed these women. They brought themselves, they did what they could, and they appear to have worked hard on behalf of the kingdom. They were a key and necessary part of Jesus' support; whether this was a front-of-house or backstage role is both unknown and immaterial. It is almost certain that they cooked, but then the male disciples used to go shopping (John 4.8). They may have had trades that they could ply on the road, but so did Paul of Tarsus (Acts 18.3;

1 Corinthians 4.12; 1 Thessalonians 2.9). Perhaps they paid out significant amounts of money, but so did Joseph of Arimathea (Mark 15.46). Perhaps – pleasant thought – one of them skilfully and seamlessly wove Jesus' tunic, so coveted by the soldiers who crucified him (John 19.23). They spent and were spent in the service of the gospel, and in this sense they provide a pattern for *all* Christian disciples.

We might ask ourselves whether Jesus was right to accept the worship – spiritual, practical and financial – of his followers. Is there any sense in which he exploited them? After all, as we have seen, some of them were vulnerable people. Jesus was the leader of what is nowadays termed a millenarian 'new religious movement',[9] and he shows *some* of the features of a 'guru':

> Gurus . . . claim the possession of special spiritual insight based on personal revelation. Gurus promise their followers new ways of self-development, new paths to salvation . . . Both recent and earlier history demonstrate that many gurus are, or become, unscrupulous wielders of power who exploit their followers in a variety of ways . . . For example, [a guru] may feel . . . that he is entitled to demand and make use of any money which his followers can raise.[10]

Throughout history the vast majority of new religious movements have been founded and led by men. In contrast, the followers are made up of both sexes, attracted by the charismatic personality of the leader. These followers often have psychological needs that are met by attachment to the group leader.[11] In his turn, it has been asserted, the leader may have his own narcissistic need to be loved and venerated by unquestioning followers.[12] On this view the narcissistic leader lives in a world of self-delusion into which reality is rarely if ever allowed to intrude. He will brook no challenge to his authority and world view. This makes him particularly vulnerable to the temptation to wield power over his disciples to meet his own wants and needs; he can easily rationalize financial or sexual exploitation away because he has, indeed allows, no 'critical friend' to help him to face the reality of his situation:

> The prophet communicates very early that there are topics that are taboo for discussion. These include his need to control others and the dependency and hero worship that are encouraged. Yes-men (or more frequently Yes-women) are installed in key positions in the group.[13]

As we have seen, Jesus was a charismatic figure – a hero – who was followed devotedly by people, many of whom had psychological needs, and to whom he promised ultimate fulfilment. He may have had a particular attraction for women.[14] He seemed to need the love of these people too. He seems to have been content to live off their earnings and to have enjoyed their hospitality. His relations with his family of origin were tense and ambivalent, and some people thought he was mad. He claimed a direct revelation from God and had a vision for a new world order. In these respects he could be described as a guru. Yet, as in so much else, Jesus seems to conform to human categories, but then turns them on their head: for Jesus is the guru who serves his followers.

In Chapter 2 we considered the way in which the Gospels emphasize the danger of misunderstanding what it means to be the Son of God. They tell the story of Jesus' struggle with the temptations to corruption that his power entails – and they indicate that Jesus faced these temptations and emerged victorious. They tell of his teaching about the way of suffering that he is destined to face, and of his repudiation of Peter who offers him what he should have wanted to hear – a rationalization for a smooth and easy way. They tell of his engagement with, not avoidance of, his critics and enemies, and of his being assertively challenged by women like Martha. They tell of his insistence that his disciples are his friends, not his servants, of his washing their feet, and his statement that servant leadership is above all *his* calling: 'For the Son of Humankind did not come to be served, but to serve and to give his life in return for many' (Mark 10.45).

Jesus' preoccupation with servanthood is a symptom of his keen awareness that power corrupts and absolute power corrupts absolutely. He knows the danger to himself and the danger to his followers, especially the men, and promises that the misuse of power in his movement will be punished (Matthew 18.23–35; Luke 12.45–46, which specifically mentions the abuse of female disciples). He speaks of it again and again. His readiness in the end to lay down his life for his sheep is a measure of his victory over the potential of power to corrupt. That is one reason why he stands so tall in relation to those men, every one corrupt, who are complicit in his execution – Herod, Annas, Caiaphas and Pilate.

Jesus depended on those women who ministered to him but he did not exploit them. He entrusted himself and his mission to their care. It was perhaps not difficult for him to do this, because from the beginning of his earthly existence he had entrusted himself to the care of a woman. He had been completely dependent on his mother's ability to carry him to term, to deliver him safely, to feed, clothe, protect and educate him. She ministered to him from her own physical, psychological and spiritual resources. As we saw in Chapter 3, given Mary's situation the odds of his safe delivery were not high. Mary seems to have been by temperament a very strong and determined woman but, according to Luke, what was driving her fundamentally were divine revelations, words – *rhēmata* – of life communicated to her by heavenly messengers and by Jesus himself (Luke 1.38; 2.19, 51). She had experienced a theophany – a special revelation of God, and she continued to be aware of the immanence of the divine in the life of her charismatic son.

Jesus' infant body was built from Mary's flesh. The Word was enabled to become flesh through Mary's consent to the divine word that had been revealed to her. Her willingness to carry and nurture the child that had been entrusted to her was her act of faith. In this she was assisted by others, especially Joseph who, according to Matthew, experienced his own theophany to fit him for the task (Matthew 1.20).

The incarnation was dependent on Mary and Joseph because God did not appear on this earth as a fully formed adult. He had a childhood. This fact is so obvious that its importance is often missed. Jesus' childhood demonstrates that childhood is important in the forming of the adult character. It is not just a phase that has to be endured while bones lengthen and reproductive equipment develops. It is a fully necessary part of the human lifespan, which could not simply be skipped when God became incarnate. In his incarnation Jesus raises men and women, but above all he raises children, and he does so very explicitly (Matthew 18.2–3 and parallels; 19.13–15 and parallels).

In childhood the beginnings of identity formation take place through a process of negotiation with the primary care-givers. Much of this is through direct interaction. Even more is through watching and imitating. Jesus will have worked out what it means to feel secure with Mary. He will have learnt to walk and talk with Mary. He will have learnt to play and to pray with Mary. He will have learnt about the work of women by watching Mary. He will have experienced the whole rough and tumble of family life with brothers and sisters, and he will have learnt too from Joseph. He entrusted himself at the deepest level to the care of a woman, and more broadly to the care of a human family.

It is relatively easy to see that the birth of Jesus required the cooperation of one human being, a woman. Mary was the primary witness to Jesus' entry into the world. More than that, she participated in the event. Indeed our concept of the 'incarnation' depends on the human participant witness of Mary. On the face of it the resurrection of Jesus is rather different, for surely Jesus rose from the grave without human help? Yet we find that a certain group of women became intimately caught up with it, and their cooperation was required to help in 'realizing' it for the Church. Our concept of the 'resurrection' depends on the human participant witness of these women.

Who has believed what we have heard? And to whom has the arm of the LORD been revealed?

And it was the day of Preparation, and the sabbath was drawing near. The women followed – those who had come together with him from Galilee – and they saw the tomb and how his body was laid. Then they went home, and prepared aromatic spices and ointments. And on the sabbath they rested according to the commandment. But on the first day, at daybreak, they came to the tomb, bringing the spices that they had prepared. They found the stone rolled away from the tomb; having gone in they did not find the body of the Lord Jesus. While they were at a loss at this – look! – two men in dazzling clothes approached them. Now they were terrified, bowing their faces to the ground; the men said to them, 'Why are you looking for the living among the dead? He is not here, on the contrary he has risen. Remember how he spoke to you, while he was still in Galilee, saying that it was necessary for the Son of Humankind to be handed over to sinful people, and to be crucified, and on the third day to rise again.' And they remembered his words. And, having returned from the tomb, they proclaimed all this to the Eleven and to all the rest. Now it was Mary Magdalene and Joanna and Mary – her of James – and the other women with them. They told this to the apostles. And these words seemed in their judgment like nonsense, and they refused to believe them . . .

'What's more, some women from among us amazed us. They were at the tomb early in the morning and, not having found his body there, they came saying that they had seen a vision of angels who say he is alive. And some of our company went to the tomb and found it just as the women had said; but him they did not see.' And he said to them, 'Oh, foolish and slow of heart to believe all that the prophets have proclaimed!'

(Luke 23.54—24.11; 24.22–25)

Jesus entrusted himself to Judas, who in his turn entrusted Jesus to others, who condemned, tortured and executed him. All those involved were men. Jesus' death on the cross was witnessed by many people, some of whom are named in the Gospels. It is also later referred to by other ancient sources.[15] Jesus was buried in a secure tomb. This was witnessed by a small group of people, predominantly women, named in the Gospels. Two days later the tomb was found empty and the body was missing. The Gospels tell us that several people saw the empty tomb. Shortly after this people – many people according to Paul (1 Corinthians 15.3–8) – experienced encounters with an individual they believed to be Jesus. The Gospels give us details of such encounters that involved conversations with Cleopas and his companion (Luke 24.15ff.), Mary of Magdala (John 20.14ff.), Thomas (John 20.27ff.) and Peter (John 21.15ff.), alongside more sketchy summaries. In all the detailed accounts, the identity of Jesus is not at first clear, but by the end of the encounter the individual has come to the conclusion that the person he or she has met is indeed Jesus. In each case some compelling psychological or physical evidence is offered. Cleopas and his companion recognize Jesus when he breaks bread, and reflect with hindsight that the way the stranger opened up the Scriptures to them on the road was characteristic of Jesus. Mary is called by name, presumably in a recognizable intonation. Peter meets with Jesus over a charcoal fire, and the threefold question and answer that follows indicates a shared memory of a threefold denial by another charcoal fire. Thomas is offered the evidence of Jesus' wounds.

139

There are pieces of a jigsaw puzzle: a dead man, an empty tomb, his earlier teaching that he would be raised, and encounters with a lovely stranger who is yet deeply familiar. Put all these together and you are in a position to reach a conclusion. Jesus died and is now alive: therefore Jesus has risen from the grave. Received in this way, the raising of Jesus is an inference, albeit one that is supported by the presence of Jesus himself.

But there is a final piece of the jigsaw puzzle that remains to be put in place. This is the fact that the women who discovered the empty tomb saw something else too. They experienced a theophany. The presence of angels described in all four Gospels is an indication of the immanence of the Lord. The women come in the dim light of early morning and they see an angel of the Lord (Matthew 28.2), or a young man dressed in white (Mark 16.5), or two young men in dazzling white (Luke 24.4), or two angels in white (John 20.12). We cannot reconstruct their experience. They clearly have come into direct contact with the divine, and they use the concepts and language of their culture to communicate what was by most accounts a terrifying incident. Luke's description of the young men is like the description of Jesus during the transfiguration (Matthew 17.2 and parallels), which is itself a foretaste of the resurrection. The glory of the Lord is shining around the women as it shone around the men on the transfiguration mount.

For these women the raising of Jesus is not an event pieced together with hindsight; its immediate aftermath is directly and dramatically witnessed. They do not see the body of Jesus rise from its resting place in any literal sense (though in John's account there is a suggestion that Mary has encountered Jesus in some kind of transition). But they do witness the power and action of God in that place. And the witnesses are given words – *rhēmata* in Luke's account – of information and instruction. In Mark's and Luke's versions the words of instruction are given them by heavenly messengers. In John's version they are given by Jesus to Mary of Magdala alone. In Matthew's version they are given by the heavenly messengers and repeated by Jesus.

The women are told to remember Jesus' teaching that he would rise (Mark 16.7; Luke 24.6–7) and to tell the other disciples that he has indeed risen (Matthew 28.7; Mark 16.7; John 20.17). In Mark's version the women are at first too scared to obey the instruction to tell others. In Luke's version they take it for granted that they should tell the others. The gist of all this is that the women are encouraged to connect what they see and hear with what Jesus taught them right from the beginning of their time following him in Galilee, and they are commissioned with a prophetic message of divine origin.

Only the women disciples see the angels. Only women are given the message. Why is this? First, as we saw in Chapter 6, there is an element of pragmatism in the kingdom of God: the women happened to be in the right place at the right time. But this is precisely because they *were* women, going about women's work. The liminal spaces between life and death – the birthing room and the tomb – are the province of women. The places of most profound mystery, the points in time and space where the incarnation and resurrection 'became' or 'happened' are women's places. Just as God entrusted himself to the care of Mary as Jesus-the-foetus, he entrusted the raw reality of his breaking out of the tomb to a group of women who were intent on caring for his broken body. His entry into the world was physically felt by his mother. His breaking out of the tomb was physically felt by these women.

The women were witnesses, and they were well qualified so to be because they had been with Jesus from the early days in Galilee. The instructions given them by the heavenly messengers emphasize this fact, and confirm their authority. When the eleven have to choose a man to replace Judas they too impose this criterion:

'. . . of the men having accompanied us all of the time that the
Lord Jesus went about among us, beginning from the baptism
of John until the day when he was taken up from us – one of
these must become a witness with us to his resurrection.'

(Acts 1.21–22)

In his book *Jesus and the Eyewitnesses*, Richard Bauckham sets
out a convincing case for the importance of this principle in the
early Church:

> . . . the most authoritative eyewitness is one who was present
> at the events narrated from their beginning to their end and
> can therefore vouch for the overall shape of the story as well as
> for specific key events. This principle highlighted the special
> significance of the Twelve but also of others who were disciples
> of Jesus for much of the period of his ministry.[16]

The women are to witness to the family of disciples (Jesus uses
the term 'brethren' when talking to Mary Magdalene). In this
quasi private and domestic sphere their testimony would have
been considered valid and authoritative,[17] no matter what the
status of their public testimony under Jewish and Roman law.[18]
Their status in the kingdom of God is clear: they are the first
witnesses of the resurrection; they are given the commission of
proclaiming the good news to the Church.

But there is more. The fact that the women are raised up in
this way is in itself a mark of the coming of the kingdom.
Throughout his earthly ministry gender pairs appear in the
life and teaching of Jesus. As we have seen, the male appears
first followed by the female. At the resurrection this order is
reversed. The females are given priority over the males. The
last are first and the first are last. When the women encounter
the angels they are not just witnessing the resurrection, they
are participating in it. The message that they receive is very
enlightening.

- First, they are aware of the immanence of God: 'You are not
  on your own.'

- Second, they are confronted with the fact that a place that they expected to be full of death is inconceivably different: 'Things don't have to be this way.'
- Finally, they are given a task of the highest importance: 'Get up and grow up!'

Mark has no more to tell us. Matthew and John indicate that the women pass on the message, but do not say how it is received. Luke goes into much more detail. He says that the women are not believed by the other disciples. The words given them by the heavenly messenger seem like nonsense. This is odd, because the message was designed to be clearly connected with the shared memory of the group. Yet it cannot be received by the community. It is as if its ears are closed. There are some resonances here with the predicament of Elizabeth, a woman of priestly heritage (Luke 1.5), who is ignored when she passes on the message of the angel that her son should be called John (1.60–63). She might as well be invisible. The crowd turn for an authoritative word on the child's name to her husband, notwithstanding the fact that he has been struck dumb for his lack of faith![19]

Despite his lack of belief, Peter goes and has a look at the tomb. He sees no angels, merely the mundane evidence of the tomb's previous occupation by Jesus. It is as if he is blind or, to use the words of Jesus on the Emmaus road, 'foolish and slow of heart to believe all that the prophets have proclaimed!' The word 'all' is exactly what the women have proclaimed to the community (Luke 24.9), and it has not been believed. Jesus seems to be rather harsh with the couple on the Emmaus road – that is, until we see that they have just told him that the first witnesses of the resurrection, the first *apostles* (an apostle is one who is sent) have not been received: 'He receiving you receives me, and he receiving me receives him who sent me. He receiving a prophet in the name of a prophet will obtain the reward of a prophet' (Matthew 10.40–41a).

But Peter's trip to the tomb has perhaps not been in vain. It has given him food for thought. This is made clear by John (John 20.6–7) as well as Luke. The message of the women has sown a little seed. That seed is there in the minds of Cleopas and his companion too. It is that seed that is the catalyst for two and two finally coming together to make four: an empty tomb, a memory of Jesus' teaching, a lovely familiar stranger and, buzzing around in the background, *a tale of angels who say that Jesus is risen.*

The women's theophany at the empty tomb is the necessary condition for the emergence of a belief in the raising of Jesus. It is the divinely disclosed piece that holds the rest of the jigsaw in place. An encounter with the risen Jesus is the sufficient condition, the final piece that makes sense of it all. It helps a lot if the encounter with Jesus is direct and physical, but this is not essential: 'Jesus said to [Thomas], "Have you believed because you have seen me? Blessed are those who have not seen and yet have come to believe"' (John 20.29, NRSV).

What we call 'the resurrection' is a complex phenomenon that is made up of a divine cosmic event involving Jesus, its divine revelation to human beings, and its reception by human beings, who are in the process themselves raised up. A group of women were uniquely integral to it and it was in this sense entrusted to them.

It is ironic that in his conversations with Mary of Magdala and Simon Peter, the risen Jesus commissions Mary to proclaim the gospel and commissions Peter to a pastoral ministry of care. For a while the authoritative position of women within the church community seems to have been maintained (Acts 12.12; 16.40; Romans 16.1, 5; 1 Corinthians 1.11; Philippians 4.2). However, the cultural constraints of the time would have excluded women from a regular proclamation ministry in secular public spaces. As the Church became less domestic and more allied to the market places and temples of Rome, and as Christianity became a religion, proclamation with its power and authority rapidly became male-only territory.[20] Pastoral care fell to the lot of females. In this light the angels' instruction to the women to remember how things had been with Jesus is both significant and poignant.

The angels' words to the women at the tomb remain compelling for all Christians. There is perhaps a particular need for Christian *women* to reappropriate them today: 'Where your brethren forget how things were with Jesus – remind them; where your brethren refuse to believe you – stand firm; where your brethren try to silence you or denigrate your message – speak out with courage; above all, keep telling your story.'

The first proclamation of the gospel was that of women, and despite the apparently rocky ground on which their words fell, they bore great fruit. The women obeyed the command of the angels. (Even Mark would concede that the women told their story eventually, otherwise how would he know of it?) In faith they did what they could, and told the truth to their community. God's trust in them was vindicated.

This is the nature of proclamation. It must be done. It is the call of all disciples to tell their stories, to witness to Christ in whatever situation they find themselves. How the story is received by others is not their primary concern; they are to broadcast widely, knowing that the seed will take root and grow in often unconventional ways and in unexpected places. The story will be a love story that is all about being needed, saved, seen, known, called, educated, entrusted and thus raised up by God's action in Jesus. It is a story of our transformation. Christ's demand on us is that, as he has treated us in this way, so are we – men and women – to treat each other; as he has raised us up, so are we to get up, grow up and live the resurrection life.

> Wisdom has built her house,
> she has hewn her seven pillars.
> She has slaughtered her animals, she has mixed her wine,
>   she has also set her table.

145

She has sent out her servant-girls, she calls
  from the highest places in the town,
'You that are simple, turn in here!'
  To those without sense she says,
'Come, eat of my bread
  and drink of the wine I have mixed.
Lay aside immaturity, and live,
  and walk in the way of insight.'
                (Proverbs 9.1–6, NRSV)

Notes

Introduction

1 T. Martin (Thérèse of Lisieux) (1898/1958) *Histoire d'une âme*, trans. R. Knox, Book 1, Chapter 1, London, Collins, p. 25.

2 By stories in this book I do not mean fiction. I mean accounts of historical events which are written and received as narratives.

3 Most scholars agree that Mark 3.13, quoted here by Thérèse, refers to the Twelve because they are identified by name in the following verses (3.14–19). Nevertheless, the meaning is ambiguous, and it is possible to read this as an account of the call of a larger group of disciples from whom the Twelve are then selected.

4 Anthropologists are sceptical about the existence of true matriarchal societies (see J. Bamberger (1974) 'The myth of matriarchy: Why men rule in primitive societies', in M. Zimbalist Rosaldo and L. Lamphere (eds) *Women, Culture, and Society*, Palo Alto, CA, Stanford University Press, pp. 263–80), but acknowledge that there are some societies where women play a prominent, if not central, role. These may be described as 'matrifocal'.

5 Women in Khasi society are the property-owners, and property passes by inheritance from mother to youngest daughter. They have a good deal of independence in relation to their husbands. A child takes the surname of its mother. A Khasi clan mother acts as community chief and priest. However, more formal government administration has traditionally been the exclusive province of males (such as my grandfather U-Ron Singh Syiem).

6 For a parallel in the Greek Old Testament see Judith 8.32 and 13.18–20.

7 See J. Duff and J. Collicutt McGrath (2006) *Meeting Jesus: Human Responses to a Yearning God*, London, SPCK, pp. 124–7.

8 In his critical approach to hermeneutics Paul Ricoeur talks of a process of 'distantiation' – letting the text be strange without prematurely trying to make sense of it, whereby I, the reader 'disappropriate myself in order to let the matter of the text be. So I

exchange the *me* (*moi*), *master* of itself, for the self (*soi*), *disciple of* the text': P. Ricoeur (1975) 'Phenomenology and hermeneutics', in J. Thompson (ed.) *Hermeneutics and the Human Sciences*, Cambridge, Cambridge University Press, p. 101. Those of us who are very familiar with certain biblical texts can have a problem with letting the text be strange in order to come humbly before it.

1 Beyond Mr Darcy

1 Selena Gray writing in *Alpha News*, number 72 (2007/8).

2 'The brain itself has been shaped and influenced by the remote experiences of mankind. But although our inheritance consists in physiological paths, still it was mental processes in our ancestors that created the paths. If these traces come to consciousness again in the individual, they can do so only in the form of mental processes, and if these processes can become conscious only through individual experience and thus appear as individual acquisitions, they are none the less pre-existing traces, which are merely "filled-out" by the individual experience. Every "impressive" experience is such an impression, in an ancient but previously unconscious stream-bed': F. Fordham (1959) *An Introduction to Jung's Psychology*, London, Penguin, p. 22. See also A. Stevens (2001) *Jung: A Very Short Introduction*, Oxford, Oxford University Press.

3 There is a clear analogy with the understanding of language pioneered by Noam Chomsky in his 1957 book *Syntactic Structures*, The Hague, Mouton. This asserts that while each language is determined by its local conditions, all languages nevertheless share the same deep meaning structure.

4 C. S. Lewis held that Christianity takes the structural form of a myth yet differs from all other such myths, because it is the real myth, to which all other myths only approximate. See C. S. Lewis (2000) 'Is theology poetry?', in *C. S. Lewis: Essay Collection and Other Short Pieces*, London, Collins, pp. 1–21.

5 A classic work in this area is J. Campbell (1949) *The Hero with a Thousand Faces*, Bollingen Series XVII, Princeton, NJ, Princeton University Press.

6 C. Pearson (1986) *The Hero Within: Six Archetypes We Live By*, New York, Harper Collins. See also C. Pearson (1991) *Awakening*

the Hero Within: Twelve Archetypes to Help us Find Ourselves and Transform the World, San Francisco, CA, Harper San Francisco.

7 C. G. Jung (1952/1967) 'Symbols of transformation: An analysis of the prelude to a case of schizophrenia', trans. R. F. C. Hull, in H. E. Read *et al.* (eds) *The Collected Works of C. G. Jung*, Vol. 5, London, Routledge and Kegan Paul.

8 The theme of a pioneer with whom we can identify is another connection with Hebrews (Hebrews 4.15; 12.2).

9 For a good account of Tolkien's use of archetypes see P. Grant (1973) 'Tolkien: Archetype and word', *Cross Currents*, pp. 365–80.

10 Extract from Johann Heerman, *Herzliebster Jesu*, 1630, trans. R. Bridges, 1899.

11 'Conviction of sin' is a technical term that arose within Puritanism for the individual's felt sense of unworthiness before God. For a detailed discussion see J. Packer (1994) *A Quest for Godliness: The Puritan Vision of the Christian Life*, Wheaton, IL, Crossway, pp. 163–76.

12 Heerman, *Herzliebster Jesu*.

13 Sarah Frantz makes the point that in Austen's cultural milieu, displaying emotion is a sign of weakness in the male. The man who is in control of his emotions is both noble and strong, and thus to be desired as a mate. (This contrast is explored most fully in the characters of Mr Edward Ferrars, Colonel Brandon and Mr Willoughby in *Sense and Sensibility*.) S. Frantz (2003) 'Jane Austen's heroes and the great masculine renunciation', *Persuasions: The Jane Austen Journal*, 25.

14 Marcus Borg, in M. Borg and N. T. Wright (1999) *The Meaning of Jesus*, London, SPCK, p. 82 (my italics).

15 A. Schweitzer (1906/1910) *The Quest of the Historical Jesus: A Critical Study of its Progress from Reimarus to Wrede*, trans. W. Montgomery, London, A & C Black.

16 Key examples include E. Renan (1863) *Vie de Jesus*; J. R. Seeley (1866) *Ecce Homo*; J. Weiss (1892) *The Preaching of Jesus and the Kingdom of God*.

17 This is one way of interpreting Philippians 2.7. Entering into human–human relationships entails a servitude to the psychological projections of the other. Moreover, taking on a human mind entails a servitude to the limitations of a human mind.

18 HOLDING OUT FOR A HERO, Dean Pitchford, Jim Steinman. © Copyright 1984 Sony/ATV Music Publishing. All rights reserved. Used by permission.

19 For a full discussion of the playfulness of God see J. Berryman (1991) *Godly Play: An Imaginative Approach to Religious Education*, San Francisco, CA, Harper San Francisco.

20 The idea that Jesus can be treated as an idol may seem strange, but both John 6.15 and 1 Corinthians 1.12 seem to be referring to something of this sort.

21 For an interesting discussion on this point see E. Schüssler Fiorenza (2000) *Jesus and the Politics of Interpretation*, London, Continuum, pp. 145ff.

2 Jesus realizes

1 Prince Charles quoted in *Time* magazine, 27 June 1969.

2 This right time refers both to the birth of Christ (Galatians 4.4) and to key points in his ministry, betrayal and death.

3 R. Baumeister (1991) *Meanings of Life*, New York, Guilford Press. For a critique of claims for the cultural universality of some of these concepts see H. Heine, H. Markus and S. Kitayama (1999) 'Is there a universal need for self esteem?', *Psychological Review*, **106**, 766–94.

4 John 12.29.

5 In light of the psychological theory that people may find in God a relationship that compensates for insecure or absent attachment figures in their early life. See L. Kirkpatrick (2005) *Attachment, Evolution, and the Psychology of Religion*, New York, Guilford Press, Chapter 6, 'God as a substitute attachment figure: The compensation hypothesis', pp. 127–45. Unlike Freud's approach, this theory does not question the reality of God, but simply explores the psychological agendas that people bring to their relationship with God.

6 See D. Capps (2000) *Jesus: A Psychological Biography*, St Louis, MO, Chalice Press, Chapter 6, 'The hidden years: The fatherhood question', pp. 129–65 for a full discussion.

7 For a discussion on Jesus as a natural theologian see A. McGrath (2008) *The Open Secret: A New Vision for Natural Theology*, Oxford, Blackwell, pp. 117–26.

8 J. Singer and P. Salovey (1993) *The Remembered Self: Emotion and Memory in Personality*, New York, The Free Press.

9 Matthew, Mark and Luke are collectively referred to as the Synoptic Gospels. The Jesus presented in John's Gospel has a much more confident and theologically 'completed' sense of his own identity. Nevertheless, there is still some sense of struggle with his destiny (John 12.27).

10 See S. Davies (1995) *Jesus the Healer: Possession, Trance, and the Origins of Christianity*, New York, Continuum, pp. 93–100 for an interesting discussion of the recognition of one spirit-filled (or 'beside himself'? – Mark 3.21–22) human being by other spirit-filled (or 'beside themselves') human beings.

11 This realization is in both senses of the word – the making real and solid (rather than the individual man Peter) is perhaps what Jesus is referring to when he talks about the rock on which he will build his Church. A minority of scholars (e.g. C. Caragounis (1990) *Peter and the Rock*, Berlin, De Gruyter) suggest this reading of Matthew 16.18.

12 The phrase commonly translated 'Son of Man' has been interpreted in a wide variety of ways by scholars. A very helpful summary of the discussions is given by James Dunn in his book *Jesus Remembered* (2003, Grand Rapids, MI, Eerdmans, Chapter 16) in which he remarks that 'the degree of complexity in the data is unparalleled in the Jesus tradition' (p. 759). He advances a very cautious historical hypothesis: Jesus used an Aramaic idiom for 'oneself' in an ambiguous way that *may* have had some connection with Daniel 7.13 and thus alluded to his future suffering and vindication.

13 See J. Duff and J. Collicutt McGrath (2006) *Meeting Jesus: Human Responses to a Yearning God*, London, SPCK, pp. 48–51 for a full discussion.

14 E. Erikson (1956) 'The problem of ego identity', *The Journal of the American Psychoanalytic Association* 4, 56–121. Reprinted in E. Erikson (1980) *Identity and the Life Cycle*, New York, Norton, pp. 108–75.

15 See Chapter 7.

16 Samaria was a hilly territory area lying to the north of Judaea and south of Galilee. (However, the main route between Galilee

and Judaea passed along the flat Jordan valley and through Jericho, avoiding Samaria, which was more difficult to traverse.) The split between its Israelite inhabitants and the Judaeans probably dates from the fourth century BC because of a dispute over the legitimate site of the Temple. The Samaritans worshipped the Lord at their temple on Mount Gerizim, overlooking Shechem, but this was destroyed by John Hyrcanus, the Hasmonean king of Judaea about 100 BC. The Samaritans took the five books of the law, the Torah, as their sacred text.

17 See Duff and Collicutt McGrath, *Meeting Jesus*, pp. 20–5.

18 For instance, Zephaniah; Isaiah 24; Amos 5; Psalms 74 and 79.

19 R. Bauckham (2006) *Jesus and the Eyewitnesses*, Grand Rapids, MI, Eerdmans.

20 R. McIver and M. Carroll (2004) 'Distinguishing characteristics of orally transmitted material when compared to material transmitted by literary means', *Applied Cognitive Psychology*, **18**, 1251–69; D. Duling (2006) 'Social memory and biblical studies: Theory, method, and application', *Biblical Theology Bulletin*, **36**, 2–4.

21 Words for enemies occur in 56 out of the 150 psalms, and for 'the wicked' in 40 out of 150. For a detailed consideration of all the Hebrew terms see H.-J. Kraus (1986) *The Theology of the Psalms*, Minneapolis, MN, Augsburg, pp. 125–66.

22 C. Rodd (2001) 'Psalms', in J. Barton and J. Muddiman (eds) *The Oxford Bible Commentary*, Oxford, Oxford University Press, pp. 356–7.

23 B. Doyle (2004) 'Howling like dogs: Metaphorical language in Psalm 59', *Vetus Testamentum*, **54**, 61–82.

24 Capernaum was in Galilee, which (unlike Judaea) was not under direct Roman administration. It was part of the territory of Herod Antipas. The centurion makes much of his *similarity* with Jesus – emphasizing that they are both men of authority. Furthermore, Luke (Luke 7.4–5) indicates that he was a 'God fearer' or proselyte. All this places him in marked contrast to the Syro-Phoenician woman.

25 I. D. Suttie (1935) *The Origins of Love and Hate*, London, Kegan Paul, Trench, Trubner & Co., pp. 127–38.

26 B. Bettelheim (1955) *Symbolic Wounds: Puberty Rites and the Envious Male*, Glencoe, IL, Free Press; N. Jay (1992) *Throughout*

Your Generations Forever: Sacrifice, Religion, and Paternity,
Chicago, IL, University of Chicago Press.

27 In *Totem and Taboo* (1913) Freud sets out his theory that the
social phenomenon of religion originated from a prehistoric
event in which a tribal group of males, in competition for females,
jealously murdered their patriarch. Religious rituals are needed
to manage the collective guilt at this dimly recalled event. There
are strong parallels with his account of the Oedipus conflict,
in which the young boy, in competition with his father for the
sexual favours of his mother, deals with his jealousy by identifying with his father. Here, argues Freud, lies the psychological
origin of belief in and devotion to a patriarchal God.

28 Nevertheless, there is some conceptual space offered for feminine
aspects of the divine afforded by the ancient Jewish wisdom
literature, to which we will return.

3 Jesus saves

1 Eusebius, the third-century bishop of Caesarea, seemingly refers
to an account of this incident when describing the (now lost)
Sayings of the Lord Explained by Papias, the early-second-century
bishop of Hierapolis, in his magisterial work *The History of the
Church*, III.39.

2 Codex Bezae is a fifth-century vellum manuscript of the New
Testament, written in both Greek and Latin. It contains most of
the four Gospels and Acts, and a fragment of 3 John.

3 'The same day, seeing someone working on the Sabbath, he said
to him, "Man, if indeed you know what you are doing then you
are blessed. But if you do not know, then you are accursed and a
transgressor of the law."'

4 R. Dawkins (2006) *The God Delusion*, London, Bantam Press,
pp. 57, 248.

5 J. D. M. Derrett (1963) 'Law in the New Testament: The story of
the woman taken in adultery', *New Testament Studies*, 10, 1–16.

6 B. Young (1995) ' "Save the adulteress!" Ancient Jewish *responsa* in
the gospels?', *New Testament Studies*, 41, 59–70.

7 For an introduction to this controversial area see F. Reilly (2005)
'Jane Schaberg, Raymond E. Brown, and the problem of the
illegitimacy of Jesus', *Journal of Feminist Studies in Religion*, 21.1,

57–80; D. Capps (2000) *Jesus: A Psychological Biography*, St Louis, MO, Chalice Press, Chapter 6, 'The hidden years: The fatherhood question', pp. 129–63.

8 Matthew tells us that Mary was 'betrothed' to Joseph. Evidence from ancient sources (the Mishnah) indicates that this involved a formal contract entered into before witnesses, giving the man rights over the girl. It could only be broken by divorce. At this point the couple may have been referred to as husband and wife, even though they did not yet cohabit or have sexual relations. Betrothal usually took place via parental agreement when the girl was aged 12 or 13, and the marriage, which involved a second public ceremony, took place a year or so later.

9 Lesser punishments involved public stripping or beating.

10 The distinction between rape and seduction often did not find its expression in real difference. The fact that the woman is no longer pure is more important than any issue of moral complicity.

11 '[Celsus] speaking of the mother of Jesus, and saying that "when she was pregnant she was turned out of doors by the carpenter to whom she had been betrothed, as having been guilty of adultery, and that she bore a child to a certain soldier named Panthera;" and let us see whether those who have blindly concocted these fables about the adultery of the Virgin with Panthera, and her rejection by the carpenter, did not invent these stories to overturn His miraculous conception by the Holy Ghost: for they could have falsified the history in a different manner, on account of its extremely miraculous character, and not have admitted, as it were against their will, that Jesus was born of no ordinary human marriage' (Origen, *Against Celsus 1*, Chapter XXXII).

12 For instance, the difference in perspectives between Matthew's and Luke's infancy narratives is striking. For a general discussion see J. C. Anderson (1983) 'Matthew: Gender and reading', in M. A. Tolbert (ed.) *The Bible and Feminist Hermeneutics, Semeia*, 28, 3–27.

13 For an introduction to the notion of honour see N. Lindisfarne (1998) 'Gender, shame, and culture: An anthropological perspective', in P. Gilbert and B. Andrews (eds) *Shame: Interpersonal Behaviour, Psychopathology and Culture*, New York, Oxford University Press, pp. 246–60.

14 As noted in the Introduction, Mary sings of the respect shown her by God in the midst of her humiliation (Luke 1.48).

15 For an interesting consideration of Tamar see E. M. Menn (1997) *Judah and Tamar (Genesis 38) in Ancient Jewish Exegesis*, Leiden, Brill.

16 See, for instance, N. Tapper (1991) *Bartered Brides*, Cambridge, Cambridge University Press; also J. Pilch (1997) 'Family violence in cross-cultural perspective: An approach for feminist inter-preters of the Bible', in A. Brenner and C. Fontaine (eds) *A Feminist Companion to Reading the Bible: Approaches, Methods and Strategies*, Sheffield, Sheffield Academic Press, pp. 306–23.

17 P. Gilbert (1998) 'What is shame: Some core issues and contro-versies', in Gilbert and Andrews, *Shame*, p. 17.

18 M. Douglas (1966) *Purity and Danger*, London, Routledge.

19 An obvious modern parallel is the public head-shaving of French women who had entered into liaisons with occupying Nazis, after France was liberated in 1945. This would be a particularly apt parallel if the woman's 'partner in crime' is absent from the scene because he is a Roman, as some have argued. This is a hypothesis advanced by J. Kim (2002) 'Adultery or hybridity? Reading John 7.53–8.11 from a postcolonial context', in M. Dube and J. Staley (eds) *John and Postcolonialism: Travel, Space, and Power*, Sheffield, Sheffield Academic Press, pp. 111–28.

20 Douglas, *Purity and Danger*, Chapter 3.

21 See M. Douglas (2004) *Jacob's Tears*, Oxford, Oxford University Press, Chapter 2, 'Jacob weeping for Joseph', pp. 38–60, for a very strong argument that 'scapegoating' is not what is happening in the Day of Atonement ritual in Leviticus 16.

22 R. Girard (1977) *Violence and the Sacred*, Baltimore, Johns Hopkins University Press. R. Girard (2003) *Things Hidden since the Foun-dation of the World*, London, Continuum.

23 Criticisms come from a variety of directions: theologians who object to the reduction of theology to anthropology; scientists who accuse Girard of peddling the Christian gospel in the guise of anthropological analysis; those who find his theory of mimesis unconvincing or overly negative.

24 It is surprising that Girard himself does not pay much attention to this story, though he does consider it in R. Girard (1995)

'Automatismes et liberté', in H. Grivoix and J.-P. Dupuy, *Mécanismes mentaux mécanismes sociaux*, Paris, Éditions La Découverte.

25 This connection was made very easily by the first Christians, who seem to have understood Susanna, a chaste wife who was falsely accused of adultery by two elders, as an ante-type of Christ. Frescoes dating from the early third century in the Priscilla catacomb in Rome seem to depict her in this way. It has even been argued that the tradition goes back as far as the gospel writers themselves: see C. Brown (2006) 'Susanna and the synoptic passion narratives', *Gregorianum*, **87**, 449–89.

4 Jesus sees

1 A classic paper in this area is C. Truax and R. Carkhuff (1965) 'Experimental manipulation of therapeutic conditions', *Journal of Consulting Psychology*, **29**, 119–24. This was a systematic examination of therapist warmth and empathic understanding on the client's ability to explore his intrapersonal issues, which found that these characteristics enhanced the client's therapeutic 'relearning'.

2 TV pictures of suffering tend to evoke a more emotional response than hearing about suffering.

3 R. Funk (1982) *Parables and Presence*, Philadelphia, PA, Fortress, p. 33 presents a very enlightening reading of the story of the good Samaritan in which 'Go and do likewise' is applied to the *victim* of the mugging, not his Samaritan helper. The listener is being exhorted to see that he is in a desperate place and must learn to receive compassion from an unexpected source. This reading makes it possible to see the stories of the prodigal son and the good Samaritan as a pair. In both the figure who stands for God sees, feels compassion, and draws near to the needy individual.

4 The verb *embrimaomai* was applied to noises made by both horses and humans; in the latter case it signifies anger.

5 This idea is elaborated by Irenaeus, the second-century bishop of Lyons, in his work, *Against Heresies*.

6 For a consideration of Jesus as eldest son see J. Miller (1997) *Jesus at Thirty: A Psychological and Historical Portrait*, Minneapolis, MN, Fortress. It is, of course, possible that Joseph had sons by a

previous marriage, in which case Jesus would not have been the eldest son in the wider Joseph clan.

7 This awareness of the sheer waste involved in the loss of their children sometimes finds its expression in movements where mothers band together aiming, like Jesus, to make things right. An example from the twentieth century is the Mothers of the Plaza de Mayo, a human rights organization made up of mothers whose children had 'disappeared' under the Argentinian dictatorship of 1976–83. A second example is the Peace People of Northern Ireland, a peace and interdenominational reconciliation movement founded by Mairead Corrigan, the aunt of three children caught in crossfire between soldiers and IRA terrorists, together with Betty Williams, a mother who witnessed their deaths. These women won the Nobel Prize for Peace in 1976.

8 They also demonstrate that parental care and grief are not confined to women: the most spectacular biblical example of a parent mourning a child is that of David mourning Absalom (2 Samuel 18.33).

9 For a feminist perspective on Matthew's use of Jeremiah see E. Wainwright (1997) 'Rachel weeping for her children: Intertextuality and the biblical testaments – a feminist approach', in A. Brenner and C. Fontaine (eds) *A Feminist Companion to Reading the Bible*, Sheffield, Sheffield Academic Press, pp. 452–69.

10 The Gospel of Thomas was probably written in Greek in the second century, though most of it is known to us only in a later Coptic translation. It contains 114 sayings attributed to Jesus, many of which have parallels in the four Gospels.

11 See J. Duff and J. Collicutt McGrath (2006) *Meeting Jesus: Human Responses to a Yearning God*, London, SPCK, Chapter 9, 'The window of opportunity', pp. 115–30 for a full discussion.

12 The theme of inversion of values in the new age is powerfully expressed by Bob Dylan in his song 'The times they are a-changin''. Copyright © 1963; renewed 1991 Special Rider Music. For an exploration of Dylan's use of biblical themes in his lyrics see M. Gilmour (2004) *Tangled up in the Bible: Bob Dylan and Scripture*, London, Continuum.

13 For an anthropological analysis see J. Sørensen (2002) 'Charisma, tradition, and ritual: A cognitive approach to magical agency', in H. Whitehouse and R. McCauley (eds) *Mind and Religion*, Lanham, MD, AltaMira Press, pp. 167–85.

14 See T. K. Seim (2002) 'The virgin mother: Mary and ascetic discipleship in Luke', in A.-J. Levine and M. Blickerstaff (eds) *A Feministic Companion to Luke*, London, Continuum, p. 90.

15 The relationship between the Great War and the advancement of women's suffrage is, however, complex. See, for instance, A. Smith (2005) *Suffrage Discourse in Britain during the First World War*, Farnham, Ashgate.

16 Carol Midgley, 'Britain is no country for old women', *The Times*, 11 December 2008, describes age discrimination in the media that affects women significantly more than men.

17 'Ted: Are you wearing your contacts? Mrs Doyle: No . . . a dog ran off with them! I thought I could get away with it but I suppose I'll HAVE to wear the glasses. I don't like wearing them, Father – they make me look like a frustrated old bag!' From G. Linehan and A. Matthews (2000) *Father Ted: The Complete Scripts*, London, Boxtree.

18 A. B. Ulanov (1977) 'The witch archetype', *Quadrant*, 10.

19 See R. Bauckham (2002) *Gospel Women*, London, Continuum, p. 100.

20 J. Salisbury (1991) *Church Fathers, Independent Virgins*, London, Verso.

21 E. Erikson, J. Erikson and H. Kivinick (1986) *Vital Involvement in Old Age*, New York, Norton; C. Jung (1931) 'The stages of life', trans. R. F. C. Hull, in H. E. Read et al. (eds) *The Collected Works of C. G. Jung*, Vol. 8, London, Routledge and Kegan Paul.

22 P. Baltes and U. Staudinger (2000) 'Wisdom: A metaheuristic (pragmatic) to orchestrate mind and virtue toward excellence', *American Psychologist*, 55, 122–36.

23 The Septuagint (Greek Old Testament) version of Proverbs 16.16 talks of wisdom's brood (*nossia*).

24 E. Schüssler Fiorenza (1994) *Jesus: Miriam's Child, Sophia's Prophet*, London, SCM Press, Chapter 5, 'Prophets of Sophia: Searching for divine wisdom', pp. 131–62.

25 Anna-Maria Rizzuto's empirical work indicates that twentieth-century people from the developed world experience God (that is, describe what she calls their personal 'God image') in terms of their relationship with early caregivers, both male and female, even if the formal teaching of their religion is predominantly patriarchal. A.-M. Rizzuto (1979) *The Birth of the Living God:*

A Psychoanalytical Study, Chicago, University of Chicago Press. See also E. Johnson (1992) *She Who Is: The Mystery of God in Feminist Theological Discourse*, New York, Crossroad, pp. 55–7.

26 J. Suggs (1970) *Wisdom, Christology, and Law in Matthew's Gospel*, Cambridge, MA, Harvard University Press, Chapter 3, 'Jesus Christ, God's wisdom and God's son', pp. 63–97.

27 For an extended consideration of Zacchaeus see Duff and Collicutt McGrath, *Meeting Jesus*.

5 Jesus knows

1 Henry in Tom Stoppard's play *The Real Thing* (1982) London, Faber & Faber, Act 2, Scene 7.

2 Or 'incomprehensible'.

3 The *persona* is a term introduced by Jung to describe the psychological 'masks' people wear to make an impression on others and conceal what he understood to be their 'true' nature (C. Jung (1935) 'The relation between the ego and the unconscious', trans. R. F. C. Hull, in H. E. Read et al. (eds) *The Collected Works of C. G. Jung*, Vol. 7, London, Routledge and Kegan Paul). For a sociological perspective on this topic see E. Goffman (1990) *The Presentation of Self in Everyday Life*, London, Penguin.

4 Enthronement sermon, Canterbury Cathedral, 27 February 2003.

5 For an interesting, if technical, discussion of this from an evolutionary perspective see J. Bering and D. Johnson (2005) 'O Lord . . . you perceive my thoughts from afar: Recursiveness and the evolution of supernatural agency', *Cognition and Culture*, 5, 118–42.

6 C. Rogers (1961) *On Being a Person*, London, Constable.

7 For more on this see J. Duff and J. Collicutt McGrath (2006) *Meeting Jesus: Human Responses to a Yearning God*, London, SPCK, pp. 2–4.

8 A classic account of this experience is given in C. S. Lewis (1998) *Surprised by Joy*, London, Fount.

9 See Chapter 2, note 16.

10 See C. Scobie (1973) 'The origin and development of Samaritan Christianity', *New Testament Studies*, **19**, 396–414 for a fascinating analysis of the evidence, and for a more elaborate account

R. Brown (1979) *The Community of the Beloved Disciple*, London, Chapman.

11 Josephus, *The Life of Flavius Josephus*, 269.

12 This is the tradition that the boy Jesus journeyed to Glastonbury in the company of his uncle, Joseph of Arimathea. The Glastonbury thorn is said to have sprouted from Joseph's staff; he left it there and it has flowered every Christmas and every spring. A cutting is in the grounds of Glastonbury Abbey.

13 R. Bauckham (2006) *Jesus and the Eyewitnesses*, Grand Rapids, MI, Eerdmans.

14 'The man called Jesus' (9.11); 'He is a prophet' (9.17); 'Who is [the Son of Man]?' (9.36); 'Lord, I believe' (9.38); 'he worshipped him' (9.38).

15 Wells were also important in the courtship of Isaac and Rebekah (Genesis 24) and Moses (Exodus 2).

16 This is an idea that can be found in the thought of Augustine of Hippo. See J. B. Elshtain (1996) *Augustine and the Limits of Politics*, Southbend, IN, University of Notre Dame Press.

17 The verb *laleō* has a technical meaning in relation to proclaiming the gospel, prophecy, or discourse on wise matters. See Matthew 12.36; 13.33; Mark 8.32; Luke 5.21; Acts 2.11; 4.29; 6.11; 1 Corinthians 2.6; 14.28; Colossians 4.3.

18 Duff and Collicutt McGrath, *Meeting Jesus*, Chapter 2, 'Drawing near', pp. 13–25.

19 Fraser Watts and Mark Williams make the point that therapeutic insight, supported by skilful therapist questioning, is in many respects similar to spiritual insight: F. Watts and M. Williams (1988) *The Psychology of Religious Knowing*, Cambridge, Cambridge University Press, pp. 70–4. For an interesting psychological perspective on Jesus and the Samaritan woman see S. Savage (2007) 'Healing encounters', in F. Watts (ed.) *Jesus and Psychology*, London, Darton, Longman and Todd, pp. 44–61.

20 Duff and Collicutt McGrath, *Meeting Jesus*, pp. 94–5.

21 Isaiah 41.4; 43.10, 13; 44.6; 46.4; 48.12; 52.6.

22 C. Williams (2000) *I Am He: The Interpretation of 'Anî Hû' in Jewish and Early Christian Literature*, Tübingen, Mohr Siebeck; D. Ball (1996) *'I am' in John's Gospel: Literary Function, Background, and Theological Implications*, Sheffield, Sheffield Academic Press. From the very beginning, John's Gospel links the creative and

redemptive work of Christ: see M. Hengel (2007) 'The prologue of the gospel of John as the gateway to christological truth', in R. Bauckham and C. Mosser (eds) *The Gospel of John and Christian Theology*, Grand Rapids, MI, Eerdmans, pp. 265–94.

6 Jesus calls

1 Scoliosis is a condition that affects more women than men from middle childhood onwards and can become progressively worse without surgical correction.

2 World Health Organization (2002) *Towards a Common Language for Functioning, Disability and Health ICF*, Geneva, World Health Organization.

3 C. Nemeroff and P. Rozin (1994) 'The contagion aspect in adult thinking in the United States: Transmission of germs and interpersonal influence', *Ethos*, 22, 158–86.

4 A patient (same root as 'passive') is essentially someone who *undergoes* things.

5 'Through the roof' is the very appropriate name of a Christian organization whose mission is 'to make the Christian message of salvation through Jesus Christ accessible to people affected by disability'; see <www.throughtheroof.org>.

6 J. Gans (1983) 'Hate in the rehabilitation setting', *Archives of Physical Medicine and Rehabilitation*, 64, 176–9.

7 M. Douglas (2002) *Purity and Danger: An Analysis of Concepts of Pollution and Taboo*, London, Routledge, Chapter 7, 'External boundaries', pp. 141–59. See also J. Duff and J. Collicutt McGrath (2006) *Meeting Jesus: Human Responses to a Yearning God*, London, SPCK, pp. 60–2.

8 The dating of the books of the law is a controversial area. For a consideration of Leviticus see G. Wenham (1995) *The Book of Leviticus*, Grand Rapids, MI, Eerdmans, pp. 8–13.

9 Vermes argues for a generally relaxed attitude to the laws in this community: G. Vermes (1973) *Jesus the Jew*, London, Collins, p. 54.

10 S. Cohen (1991) 'Menstruants and the sacred in Judaism and Christianity', in S. Pomeroy (ed.) *Women's History and Ancient History*, Chapel Hill, University of North Carolina Press, pp. 273–300.

11 For more details on the Pharisees see A. Saldirini (2001) *Pharisees, Scribes, and Sadducees in Palestinian Society*, Grand Rapids, MI, Fortress.

12 M. Douglas (1999) *Leviticus as Literature*, Oxford, Oxford University Press, Chapter 6, 'Atonement for sick bodies', pp. 176–94.

13 BBC *Newsnight*, 16 June 2003.

14 For instance, Stephen Bates: 'he startlingly expatiated on gynaecology . . .' (*The Guardian*, 18 June 2003).

15 B. Bettelheim (1955) *Symbolic Wounds: Puberty Rites and the Envious Male*, Glencoe, IL, Free Press.

16 Some feminist readings of this text hold the term 'daughter' to indicate the subordinate position of women. See, for instance, M. A. Tolbert (1998) 'Mark', in C. Newson and S. Ringe (eds) *The Women's Bible Commentary*, London, SPCK, pp. 350–62. However, this seems unnecessary given that the term 'daughter' of Abraham is used to refer to entitlement in Luke 13.16.

17 J. Wilkinson (1998) *The Bible and Healing*, Grand Rapids, MI, Eerdmans, p. 12.

18 Duff and Collicutt McGrath, *Meeting Jesus*, pp. 20–5.

19 Morna Hooker applies the concept of interchange to Paul's understanding of the believer being in Christ and Christ being in the believer (Romans 8.10; 2 Corinthians 5.17), a mutual participation through which the believer identifies with Christ by faith, and thus enjoys all the benefits due to him (Romans 6.3ff.): M. Hooker (1971) 'Interchange in Christ', *Journal of Theological Studies*, 22, 349–61; M. Hooker (1981) 'Interchange and suffering', in W. Horbury and B. McNeil (eds) *Suffering and Martyrdom in the New Testament*, Cambridge, Cambridge University Press, pp. 70–83.

20 For a detailed consideration see W. Vanstone (1982) *The Stature of Waiting*, London, Darton, Longman and Todd.

21 Hooker, 'Interchange in Christ', p. 351.

22 A. Davis (1986) *A Very Peculiar Practice*, London, Hodder & Stoughton, p. 20.

23 The case of the woman with the curved spine may seem to be an exception to this rule (Luke 13.11–16) but see Wilkinson, *The Bible and Healing*, pp. 131–41 for a detailed argument that this woman does not have a demon.

24 J. Barrett (2004) *Why Would Anyone Believe in God?*, Walnut Creek, CA, AltaMira Press, Chapter 1, 'What does it mean to "believe"?', pp. 1–19.

25 The 'Second Temple' period refers to the time after the return from the Babylonian exile, when a temple to replace Solomon's Temple was built (c. 515 BC), as described in Ezra, up until its reconstruction by Herod the Great and subsequent destruction by the Romans in AD 70. Most of the Old Testament dates from before this period, and so it tells us little about the distinctive and significant developments in Jewish culture and thought that took place over these centuries.

26 C. Rowland (1982) *Christian Origins*, London, SPCK, Chapter 3, 'The heavenly host', pp. 33–4.

27 However, this confident biological approach to mental health is disputed. See, for instance, R. Bentall (2004) *Madness Explained: Psychosis and Human Nature*, London, Penguin.

28 American Psychiatric Association (1994) *Diagnostic and Statistical Manual of Mental Disorders IV-TR*, Washington DC, American Psychiatric Association.

29 For a full discussion see C. Helman (2000) *Culture, Health and Illness*, London, Hodder Arnold, Chapter 10, 'Cross-cultural psychiatry', pp. 170–201.

30 L. Thompson (2007) *Agatha Christie: An English Mystery*, London, Headline.

31 Interestingly the APA recognizes what it calls 'trance' or 'possession' states as types of dissociative disorder, but only when they are abnormal for the affected individual's culture. For a full discussion see K. Lowenthal (2006) *Religion, Culture and Mental Health*, Cambridge, Cambridge University Press, Chapter 7, 'Dissociation', p. 105.

32 Hysteria is a term, as two experts have put it, that is 'now banned from the lexicon'. They go on to note that 'The uncertainties surrounding what constitutes hysteria still bedevil [its] purposely contrived successors': S. Lynn and J. Rhue (1994) *Dissociation: Clinical and Theoretical Perspectives*, New York, Guilford Press, p. 81.

33 E. Showalter (1987) *The Female Malady: Women, Madness, and English Culture*, New York, Virago, p. 129, citing E. Tilt (1881) *A Handbook of Uterine Therapeutics and of Diseases of Women*, New York, William Wood, p. 85.

34 J. Breuer and S. Freud (1950) *Studies in Hysteria*, trans. A. A. Brill, Boston, Beacon Press.

35 I. Lewis (1985) *Religion in Context*, Cambridge, Cambridge University Press, p. 39. This is cited in S. Davies (1995) *Jesus the Healer: Possession, Trance, and the Origins of Christianity*, New York, Continuum, in the context of a discussion on the emergence of demon possession in disempowered individuals as a response to family pressures.

36 J. Chu and D. Dill (1990) 'Dissociative symptoms in relation to childhood physical and sexual abuse', *The American Journal of Psychiatry*, 147, 887–92.

37 P. Horsfield (1998) 'The Gerasene demoniac and the sexually violated', in C. Adams and M. Fortune (eds) *Violence Against Women and Children: A Christian Theological Sourcebook*, New York, Continuum, p. 143. See C. Myers (1988) *Binding the Strong Man*, Maryknoll, NY, Orbis, pp. 190–4 for an analogous political reading.

38 For a careful consideration of gender differences in issues facing survivors of sexual abuse see R. Ganzewoort (2006) 'Masculinity and post-traumatic spirituality', paper presented at the International Colloquium on Christian Religious Education in Coping with Sexual Abuse, convened by J.-G. Nadeau, Montreal, <www.ruardganzewoort.nl/pdf/2006_Masculinity.pdf> retrieved 14 May 2009.

39 E. de Boer (2002) 'The Lukan Mary Magdalene and the other women following Jesus', in A.-J. Levine (ed.) *A Feminist Companion to Luke*, Sheffield, Sheffield Academic Press, p. 148.

40 E. Schüssler Fiorenza (1983) *In Memory of Her: A Feminist Theological Reconstruction of Christian Origins*, London, SCM Press, p. 32.

41 H. Small (1998) *Love's Madness: Medicine, the Novel, and Female Insanity, 1800–1865*, Oxford, Clarendon Press, p. 3.

42 Davies, *Jesus the Healer*, p. 95.

43 The Hebrew word here, *qûm*, is the same root as the Aramaic word used by Jesus when he addresses Jairus' daughter.

7 Jesus teaches

1 J. Duff and J. Collicutt McGrath (2006) *Meeting Jesus: Human Responses to a Yearning God*, London, SPCK, pp. 2–3.

2 Erotic imagery was a feature of much medieval mysticism, for instance in the writings of the eleventh-century Cistercian Bernard of Clairvaux.

3 J. Bowlby (1978) *Attachment and Loss, Vol. 1: Attachment*, Harmondsworth, Penguin.

4 M. Ainsworth (1993) 'Attachments and other affectional bonds across the life cycle', in V. Parkes, J. Hinde and P. Morris (eds) *Attachment Across the Life Cycle*, London, Routledge, p. 37.

5 Duff and Collicutt McGrath, *Meeting Jesus*, pp. 74–9.

6 E. Schüssler Fiorenza (1986) 'A feminist critical interpretation for liberation: Martha and Mary (Luke 10.38–42)', *Religion and Intellectual Life*, 3, 16–36.

7 For a discussion of what is meant by *diaconia*, usually translated 'serving', when applied to Martha, see W. Carter (2002) 'Getting Martha out of the kitchen: Luke 10.38–42 again', in A.-J. Levine (ed.) *A Feminist Companion to Luke*, Sheffield, Sheffield Academic Press, pp. 218–27.

8 H. Nouwen (1997) *Bread for the Journey*, London, Darton, Longman and Todd, p. 85.

9 R. Greenleaf and L. Spears (2002) *Servant Leadership: A Journey into the Nature of Legitimate Power and Greatness*, Mahwah, NJ, Paulist Press.

10 Matthew 20.20–21 seems to attribute this to the 'pushy mother syndrome', an elaboration of Mark's narrative where the culprits are clearly James and John themselves (Mark 10.35). However, on closer reading of Matthew's version, while the request is made by the mother, Jesus responds to *her sons*: 'You [plural] do not know what you [plural] are asking', and we are told that the other ten males were angry with the brothers, not their mother, indicating that the brothers put her up to it.

11 Luke's name for the Twelve.

12 This saying, 'The greatest among you will be your servant', occurs in the polemical speech directed at the scribes and the Pharisees (all men). The criticisms of these men are addressed to the whole crowd (Matthew 23.1), but the instructions for a holy life are probably addressed to an inner circle of 'his disciples'.

13 See A. Eagly and L. Carli (2007) *Through the Labyrinth: The Truth about how Women Become Leaders*, Boston, MA, Harvard Business School Press, pp. 36–7, for a review of a range of empirical

studies in this area. See also J. Sidanius and F. Pratto (1999) *Social Dominance: An Intergroup Theory of Social Hierarchy and Oppression*, New York, Cambridge University Press.

14 Eagly and Carli, *Through the Labyrinth*, p. 37.

15 See, for instance, E. Schüssler Fiorenza (1992) *But She Said: Feminist Practices of Biblical Interpretation*, Boston, Beacon Press, pp. 72–3; P. Perkins (1992) 'Philippians', in C. Newsom and S. Ringe (eds) *The Woman's Bible Commentary*, London, SPCK.

16 T. K. Seim (1994) *The Double Message: Patterns of Gender in Luke–Acts*, Sheffield, Continuum, pp. 246–68.

17 For an interesting perspective see H. Maccoby (2003) *Jesus the Pharisee*, London, SCM Press.

18 J. Coakley (1988) 'The anointing at Bethany and the priority of John', *Journal of Biblical Literature*, **107**, 241–56.

19 M. Pope, 'Euphemism and dysphemism in the Bible', *Anchor Bible Dictionary*, **1**, 720–5.

20 Greeting card caption from Emotional Rescue Limited, Cheltenham.

21 On 21 May 2009 the British Home Secretary announced that Gurkhas who retired before 1997 will be given settlement rights. This was in response to a relentless campaign fronted by the actress Joanna Lumley.

22 For material shared between Matthew and Luke but not Mark, often referred to as the 'double tradition' or 'Q', it is generally thought that Matthew edits his source in places, whereas Luke preserves it. Here this would make sense. Men lying on couches come across as lazy, and might be subject to speculation about the propriety of their behaviour – better to place them in the field.

23 A correspondence in *The Guardian* newspaper on this text evoked by the debate around the proposed appointment of Dr Jeffrey John as bishop of Reading concluded with a letter from me making this point: 'The bishop and the Bible-Bashers', 24 June 2003.

24 Some feminist commentators (for instance, S. Durber (1992) 'The female reader and the parables of the lost', *Journal for the Study of the New Testament*, **45**, 59–78) have argued that the woman is a second-class version of the shepherd because she is confined to the home, has only ten coins rather than 100, and her girls-only party is compared to the rejoicing of angels (Luke 15.10) rather than the rejoicing of God himself. But this interpretation has been strongly contested by others, for instance C. LaHurd (2002)

'Re-viewing Luke 15 with Arab Christian women', in A.-J. Levine, *A Feminist Companion to Luke*, pp. 247–68.

25 K. Bailey (1980) *Through Peasant Eyes*, Grand Rapids, MI, Eerdmans, p. 148.

26 Duff and Collicutt McGrath, *Meeting Jesus*, p. 46.

8 Jesus entrusts

1 C. Rossetti, 'In the bleak midwinter', 1872.

2 'The prayer of humble access', The Book of Common Prayer, 1662, but dating from 1548. Extracts from The Book of Common Prayer, the rights in which are vested in the Crown, are reproduced by permission of the Crown's Patentee, Cambridge University Press.

3 A. M. Toplady, 'Rock of ages', 1776.

4 K. Pargament (1997) *The Psychology of Religious Coping: Theory, Research, Practice*, New York, Guilford Press; J. Collicutt McGrath (2008) 'God's outrageous grace', in J. Duff and C. Dell (eds) *Guidelines*, **24**(3), Abingdon, Bible Reading Fellowship, pp. 86–93.

5 Some manuscripts read 'him'. For a detailed discussion of this textual issue see C. Ricci (1994) *Mary Magdalene and Many Others: Women who Followed Jesus*, trans. P. Burns, Minneapolis, MO, Fortress Press, pp. 156–8.

6 R. Bauckham (2002) *Gospel Women: Studies of the Named Women in the Gospels*, Chapter 5, 'Joanna the apostle', pp. 109–93.

7 See Bauckham, *Gospel Women*, pp. 113–17 for an excellent and thorough discussion on *ta huparchonta tini*. Also D. C. Sim (1989) 'The women followers of Jesus: The implications of Luke 8.1–3', *Heythrop Journal*, **30**, 51–62.

8 J. Collins (1990) *Diakonia: Re-interpreting the Ancient Sources*, New York, Oxford University Press, p. 60; E. de Boer (2002) 'The Lukan Mary Magdalene and the other women following Jesus', in A.-J. Levine (ed.) *A Feminist Companion to Luke*, Sheffield, Sheffield Academic Press, p. 141.

9 Millenarianism is the belief by a religious, social or political group or movement in a coming major transformation of society, after which all things will be changed. See S. Porter (2001) 'Millenarian thought in the first century church', in S. Hunt (ed.) *Christian Millenarianism from the Early Church to Waco*, London, C. Hurst, pp. 62–76.

10 A. Storr (1996) *Feet of Clay: A Study of Gurus*, New York, Simon & Schuster, pp. xi, xvi.

11 S. Murken and S. Namini (2007) 'Childhood familial experiences as antecedents of adult membership in new religious movements: A literature review', *Nova Religio*, **10**, 17–37.

12 Narcissism is a psychological characteristic where the individual's primary object of love is himself. The relationship of male narcissism to charismatic leaders has been extensively explored by the psychoanalyst Hans Kohut. See, for instance, H. Kohut (1976) 'Creativeness, charisma and group psychology: Reflections on the self-analysis of Freud', in J. Gedo and G. Pollock (eds) *Freud: The Fusion of Science and Humanisms. The Intellectual History of Psychoanalysis*, New York, International Universities Press. See also M. Weber (1968) *On Charisma and Institution Building*, Chicago, University of Chicago Press.

13 L. Oakes (1997) *Prophetic Charisma: The Psychology of Revolutionary Religious Leaders*, Syracuse, NY, Syracuse University Press, p. 15.

14 S. Freyne (2000) 'Jesus the wine-drinker: A friend of women', in I. Kitzberger (ed.) *Transformative Encounters: Jesus and Women Re-viewed*, Leiden, Brill, pp. 177–9.

15 Josephus, *Jewish Antiquities*, 18: 63–64; Tacitus, *Annals*, 15: 44, 2–3.

16 R. Bauckham (2006) *Jesus and the Eyewitnesses*, Grand Rapids, MI, Eerdmans, p. 146.

17 J. R. Wegner (1988) *Chattel or Person? The Status of Women in the Mishnah*, New York, Oxford University Press.

18 This is a controversial area. See Bauckham, *Gospel Women*, pp. 268–77 for a detailed discussion.

19 A more humble example is provided by Rhoda, who is told that she is mad when she announces the arrival of Peter (last seen in prison) to the community (Acts 12.13–15).

20 Turid Karlsen Seim charts the increasing limits placed on the freedom opened up to women in the early Church in *The Double Message: Patterns of Gender in Luke–Acts*, Edinburgh, T & T Clark, 1994. For a consideration of possible tensions between followers of Mary Magdalene and followers of Peter in the early Church see A. Graham Brock (2003) *Mary Magdalene, the First Apostle: The Struggle for Authority*, Harvard, MA, Harvard University Press.

Index of biblical references

Index of biblical references